DON,
FOR THE GOOD
OLD DIVING TIMES

Chuck Nicklin

CAMERA MAN

Stories of My Life and Adventures
as an **Underwater Filmmaker**

CHUCK NICKLIN

FIRST EDITION, OCTOBER 2015

Published in the United States by Nicklin Publications.

The Library of Congress has cataloged this edition as follows:

Nicklin, Charles 1927, September 3 -
Camera Man /by Charles Nicklin—1ˢᵗ U.S. ed.
ISBN: 978-1517383121
© 2015 by Nicklin Publications
All rights reserved. First edition 2015
Printed in the United States of America
Book cover and interior design by Doreen Hann
Cathryn Castle, editor
cathryncastle.com

Dedication

'm fortunate to have enjoyed the love and support of many people throughout my life. I wish I could acknowledge every single individual, but I am grateful to each of you for your love and support.

One person whom I must acknowledge is my wife Roz. I knew she was special the first time I saw her in a grocery store parking lot. Roz and I dated on and off for 22 years before finally marrying. We have been married for over 24 years now, and we often say, "Why did we wait so long?"

My career took me away from home for long stretches of time, but Roz supported me every minute. Sharing our lives together has made me a very happy man.

I dedicate this book and my life to Rosalind Bailey Nicklin —my amazing Roz.

Don - glad we finally connected!!
Enjoy, Roz

Table of Contents

Foreword

By Al Giddings

The task of writing something considerably more than adequate about Chuck Nicklin's decades of undersea accomplishments has proven a challenge!

According to Webster's Dictionary, the word challenge means, "demanding all of one's abilities in a stimulating way."

Chuck Nicklin's pioneering years as a premier undersea photographer span more than five decades and include hundreds of historic firsts. I pray what follows carries the full weight of his accomplishments.

Chuck and I met in 1962 on a crowded beach in La Jolla, California. Chuck was tall, handsome and sported a dynamite smile and vise-like handshake. That day we both carried spear guns and patiently waited for the National Spearfishing competition to start. In the early '60s we both owned modest underwater cameras but gave little thought to earning a living taking underwater photographs. That would soon change and photography would become a passion beyond our dreams.

As our friendship matured through the '60s, I realized full measure that beyond Chuck's engaging ways and broad smile was a superb athlete. It became obvious that Chuck was totally at ease in the sea. Equipped with only a mask and swim fins, Chuck could comfortably spear a rockfish in 80 feet of water or take a picture at twice that depth with scuba gear. Few in those early days could match Chuck's aquatic skills and watermanship—abilities that would serve him in the future in ways beyond his imagination.

By the early '70s I was producing documentary films about the wonders of the underwater world. Very often, Chuck and I worked in deep, dangerous open sea conditions, in frigid waters where visibility was only a few meters. With Chuck on board, I committed to dicey projects like filming the wreck of the *Andrea Doria* lying in 220 feet of water. The *Andrea Doria* dives demanded a brave heart and cool head. In those early days, Chuck was at the top of his game and took on the *Doria* challenge with a fearless, smart attitude. I rarely worried about him, as he instinctively knew when to hold and when to back off.

During those formative years, we worked shoulder-to-shoulder as we recorded endless firsts for Emmy awarded shows on great white sharks, humpback whales and lost Japanese Warships in Truk Lagoon. One of our more riveting encounters took place in Hawaii while trying to film elusive humpbacks. The day was stunning, the water crystal clear. Out in the deep blue less than 100 feet away, a 40-ton mother and newborn calf hung motionless in the water column. My heart pounded as I held my breath and drifted toward the pair, camera rolling. Mother and calf soon filled my frame! At touching distance and with my film roll spent, I eased under the pair as the mother whale slowly guided her newborn forward and away. Red in the face and desperate for a breath, I exhaled, knowing my shot was a stunning, detailed first! I was beyond thrilled. As I turned toward the boat, I noticed Chuck. Somehow he had skillfully settled into a prime angle and filmed the spectacular encounter with his super-wide camera. Months later in a dark editing room, I smiled, shaking my head as I cut the sequence. Without a doubt, my coverage of the whales was riveting. However, Chuck's take was clearly the stunning super master. By including me in the shot, his was the angle that provided spectacular perspective and scale! Clearly, Chuck's angle was the "money shot."

By the late '70s, Chuck and I shared the first of many Hollywood adventures. United Artists funded a "B" movie called *Sharks' Treasure*, staring Cornel Wilde. We got the call. Cornel proved to be a brave actor, so with my fingers crossed, Chuck and our underwater unit and I flew to Australia and filmed some very wild shark frenzies and zany shark cage close-ups of Cornel. As they say in Hollywood, *Sharks'*

Camera Man

Treasure "didn't play," meaning it wasn't a blockbuster. But our wild, open sea shark action registered with executives at Columbia Pictures, who were in the early production stages of one of novelist Peter Benchley's stories. We got hired. And in 1976, the motion picture *The Deep* went through the roof, grossing 130 million for Columbia Pictures. Suddenly Stan Waterman, Chuck and I were heroes, top guns in tinseltown. Chuck's camera work in the challenging Panavision wide-screen theatrical format was, as always, stunning.

Soon other Hollywood features came our way. In the '80s the James Bond films were hot. *For Your Eyes Only* featured major underwater drama, as did *Never Say Never Again*, which starred Sean Connery and Kim Basinger. Chuck and I, with our crews, had the time of our lives—and the paydays were especially sweet!

In the late '80s, legendary producer Peter Guber and I pitched and landed a five-hour CBS television series called *Ocean Quest*. Soon dozens of people were hired and, with Chuck at my side, our production team hit the road for what became a two-year global filming marathon. The *Ocean Quest* series aired in prime time on five consecutive Sunday nights—with ratings that eclipsed the wildly popular program *20/20* on two occasions.

In 1988 I received a call from film director Jim Cameron asking if we could meet and review a major feature he was planning with Fox Pictures. Within weeks we had a deal and *The Abyss* was launched. Without a doubt, it was the most demanding, ambitious underwater production ever attempted. My first call was to Chuck. With him onboard, I gathered dozens of other seasoned vets. Working 12 to 15 hour nights in an underwater set the size of a football stadium, we burned through 10,460 tanks of air in 91 nights. *The Abyss* remains, for both Chuck and me, the toughest underwater project ever. We staggered home.

In October, 2015 two fully-loaded 53-foot semis arrived at Rutgers University Marine Science Institute, each truck carrying over 8,000 pounds of film negative and original recordings—a priceless record spanning the first half century of undersea exploration. When digitized, the Rutgers library will preserve countless undersea discoveries and be available to the science community worldwide. Chuck Nicklin's contribution to this unprecedented body of work lies at the core of the Rutgers collection. It is further testament to the value of Chuck's stunning work with an undersea camera.

When asked to write a foreword for Chuck's book, I believed it to be an easy task. After all, since we have lived so many riveting and historic underwater adventures together, I'd have plenty of material. But once I started to write, a real challenge loomed: how do I distill his lifetime of innovation and accomplishments into just a few pages—and how will my words pay full tribute to Chuck's incredible achievements?

What I've written touches only the bare surface of Chuck's stellar accomplishments, which I'm sure you'll learn as you delve further into his story through the pages of this book. What we learned together, captured on film, and shared with the world, has carried personal rewards beyond our dreams. Our partnership has been a spectacular and thrilling ride. It's a ride I cherish and will forever be thankful for.

Foreword

By Flip Nicklin

I have been fortunate to have a father in whose footsteps I was happy to follow, from Chuck's Market in East San Diego to the Diving Locker in Pacific Beach, to traveling the world as a photographer, especially photographing whales. I grew up in a world hungry for adventure in the ocean. The first adventure with my father that I remember took place at La Jolla Cove, not surprisingly, as my family spent an amazing amount of time there. There was a rock offshore, "The Rock" shallow enough for people to stand on and, when the swell was right, maybe catch a body surfing wave. I can still recall hanging onto his shoulders and looking down at the marine world that came into focus through the lens of my little green dive mask. We were hardly far from shore, but that didn't make that first experience any less of an adventure.

My brother Terry and I started working with my father at the Diving Locker before we were teenagers. My Dad was not yet a serious photographer or cinematographer, but he was a heck of a diver, and a model of what a diver should be. And he was great with people. The dive shop was a haven for scientists, military divers, commercial divers, spearfishermen, and all kinds of characters in general. Years later this introduction to diversity served me well, when I was traveling the world on assignment as a photographer for *National Geographic* magazine. Chuck got along with everyone. He still does. I often find myself traveling in places he has been, and since he's so loved and respected people assume I might be okay, too. His success in diving, photography, and world travel are a result of that mix of skill and experience in the ocean and a warm personality that welcomes all and makes people feel happy to be around him.

This book is especially welcome because he has great stories to tell and because we weren't always sure he'd be willing to tell them. You see, for a long time Chuck avoided talking about what he had done, preferring to talk only about what he planned to do next. That's his nature. I see how that kept him looking toward the future—he claims it's part of what has kept him young in spirit—but so many of us are thrilled that he's finally decided to share his stories. I know I am.

For instance, once upon a time in 1963 my father sat on a whale. It happened while Chuck and his friends were out on a dive trip. He had inherited an underwater movie camera and still camera, which he was still getting used to, and he took them along on the trip, although back then the main focus was probably to catch some dinner. While cruising off La Jolla they spotted a whale at the surface. As they slowly maneuvered the boat to get a closer look, the whale didn't move. That's when they noticed it was caught in a gill net. Chuck and a dive buddy jumped in the water with the whale and freed it from the net. But before he freed the whale, Chuck climbed atop its back and just sat there for a few moments enjoying the adventure—and from then on he became known as the first man ever to ride a whale.

It would have been a great story to tell back on shore, but Chuck had those cameras, and he brought back still photos and film footage—another first. The media ate the story up. Chuck's exploits were heralded in newspapers, and the footage was shown on a late-night variety show in San Diego (hosted by a young Regis Philbin). This eventually led to my father appearing on *To Tell the Truth,* a prime-time celebrity game show. My father was now regarded as a whale expert. And the rest, as they say, is history.

I don't think either of us could have imagined what a big part of our lives these magnificent creatures would become. If you want to know more about my father's adventures as a whale expert and underwater filmmaker, just keep reading.

Acknowledgement

I first met Al Giddings at a barbecue at the home of Ron Church after a spearfishing competition in La Jolla. All three of us were good spearfishermen. Ron was one of the best. Back then Al owned Bamboo Reef, a dive shop in northern California and I was involved with the Diving Locker in San Diego. Al and I shared several common interests—spearfishing, scuba diving and underwater photography. Our friendship was immediate.

Al was just starting to make a name for himself as an underwater filmmaker. He mentioned he had just finished work on a film called *The Painted Reefs of Honduras* and was planning a new film for US Divers, *Twilight Reef*, to be shot in Cozumel.

Around this time our group, the Scientific Diving Consultants, which started the Diving Locker, was organizing the first San Diego Underwater Film Festival. I suggested that we invite Al Giddings to come to San Diego and show *Painted Reefs*. He graciously accepted the invitation.

When Al and I met at the film festival he suggested that I join him in Cozumel. I thanked him for the offer, but declined, saying it would not be possible, since I had the Diving Locker to manage, and my then-wife Gloria and I owned a small market, which we were trying to sell. A few days later I had a phone call from Al. He was insistent—he really wanted me to come work on this film with him. When I finished the phone call, I mentioned the conversation to Gloria. She said, "I think you need to do this. It sounds like a chance you shouldn't pass up. Just do it. We'll figure out some way to make things work here while you're gone."

So, I took the chance. And for the next 50 some-odd years I've worked as a cameraman on many of Al's film projects. (But you probably already knew that.)

Al and I became more than just friends. We spent a lot of time together and we made many deep dives together. Often as divers prepare for a deep dive there is a quiet time at the back of the boat, a time for calming the mind and focusing. At other times there'd be conversations, the somber kind that started with "What if … ?" Al and I always agreed that if anything goes bad underwater, we each were to save ourselves. Except that I knew Al would never leave me and I am certain I would never leave him. We've always had each other's back. Always will.

Preface

When you think about how a book gets written, you might imagine that it happens because the writer actually wanted to sit down and write the thing. It'd make sense to think like this.

But in my case, it's not what happened. Like so many other things in my life, this whole "book thing" came about because I received encouragement from my friends—friends who, when we'd be sitting down sharing stories after a day of diving, would say, "Chuck, you should write a book." Seeing as how my age clock is winding down I started thinking maybe I'd put some stories on paper in a spiral notebook to leave for my granddaughter, Grace Nicklin. But that was about it.

My wife Roz suggested I start by recording my stories. She encouraged me to take my Zoom recorder and go down to a quiet spot near the beach and just talk into the recorder, telling the stories of my life as they came to mind. So, that's what I did. Over a period of several months I ended up with seven hours of recordings, which we had transcribed. I sorted through the transcript and Roz edited it for me. I figured the "book thing" was pretty much done.

Then one night at dinner with our friends Howard and Michele Hall, Michele mentioned that I should talk with Cathryn Castle, an accomplished diver and writer/editor. Michele insisted Cathryn would be able to help me turn my collection of stories into a "real" book. So, we met with Cathryn. We hit it off right away and in a series of conversations with her we went from talking about "this book thing" to actually deciding, "Let's do this thing. Let's publish a book."

The title, *Camera Man* is a bit of a play on words. While I made a good living as a *cameraman*—which is spelled as one word—the book title reflects the fact that what I've cobbled together here is a collection of stories about my life. With—and without—a camera. Some of the stories told here are of exciting scuba diving adventures and my work as a cameraman for major motion pictures. Other stories are merely recollections from my childhood.

Still other stories are ones told by friends who've kindly agreed to contribute guest essays. I am especially grateful to all those who took the time to add to my collection.

Over the course of my long life I've accumulated many memories and stories. How lucky I am to share them with my granddaughter Grace, my family and friends, and you.

Chuck Nicklin
September 3, 2015

Cathryn Castle, Chuck, Michele Hall and Roz, revealing Chuck's book cover art at Scuba Show 2015 in Long Beach, CA.

Camera Man

"Explore into the unknown, which will always bring new and exciting adventures."

~ Roz Nicklin

"I think I'm done ..."

When I first started college in the mid-1940s I went out to the beach as much as I could, and I became very interested in freediving. At this time, the only dive gear available was military-issue equipment. Diving and snorkeling weren't sports yet, and there really wasn't such a thing a dive shop back then. I had a relative that worked with the Navy's Underwater Demolition Team or UDT, and he got me some UDT fins. They were heavy black fins like the "retro style" lifeguards wear now. I had a hard rubber mask that we ground down around the edges so it would fit my face. When I wasn't at school or at work, I'd be at the beach. Like so many southern Californians, the beach—and being in the ocean—became an important part of my life.

I got pretty good at freediving and hunting for lobster or abalone. I never missed the first day of abalone season, which was in March. My dive friend Bob Casebolt would meet me at North Bird and we'd go out hunting for abalone. We didn't have to go very far. They were everywhere. We were always trying to talk my then- wife Gloria and Bob's wife Cynthia into meeting us and cooking on the beach. It sounded more adventurous to bring catch out of the sea and enjoy it right there on the beach, but the weather in March was mostly cold, windy and crappy, so, we usually ended up having our abalone dinners at home. I guess the ladies had a bit more common sense than we did back then ...

Then came spearfishing. I'd go with a long pole spear, and I'd swim out to the kelp and try and shoot kelp bass. I loved the excitement of it. I was enjoying it, especially after meeting guys like Wally Potts and Jack Prodanovich, who were some of the early leaders in spearfishing.

I built a spear gun and brought it on a trip to Cabo San Lucas. We took a twin-engine prop plane there once, staying at the Hacienda

Hotel, which was the only hotel in town. There was no yacht club at that time but there was a cannery. At the cannery, they'd take the refuse from the canning and dump it in the water at the end of the pier. That attracted a lot of little fishes, and the little fishes would attract bigger fishes. It would attract the barracudas. Pretty soon, the big amberjacks, which they called *pez fuerte*, were coming after the barracudas. We landed 100-pound amberjacks at Cabo San Lucas. We went to La Paz a couple of times after that, going out on a boat. Dick Adcock had a boat that was sort of a live-aboard—although it was nowhere near what a diver would call a live-aboard today. It wasn't much for living, but it was a way to get out to the reefs. We had some good times diving out of La Paz. The boat was called the *Marlissa*, named after Dick's wife.

Before long I got into spearfishing competitions. I was on the Delta Divers diving team, and we were in many competitions and we did well. We'd be out in the cold water for four hours at a stretch—and we'd be doing some pretty deep dives. The good thing is we looked after each other and made sure no one passed out before reaching the surface.

Over the years I taught both my sons, Flip and Terry, to freedive and spearfish. In fact, when they were teenagers, around 14 and 15, both won the Pacific Coast Spearfishing Championship as a team.

Over time, Navy-surplus scuba gear started showing up. I was eager to try it. George Zorillo was a member of the Delta Divers and he took me on my first dive. George wasn't an instructor and there wasn't anything like a formal class back then. He just took me to La Jolla Shores and strapped a single 38-cubic foot tank to my back and taught me how to breathe through the double-hose US Divers Aqua Lung regulator. He warned me not to hold my breath and he showed me how to clear my mask, and off we went.

Our scuba gear equipment was crude—and downright dangerous—by today's standards. We had no submersible pressure gauges to

Camera Man

determine how much air was in the tank. When it became hard to breathe you headed to the surface. Running out of air was a common occurrence, so we became good at emergency ascents.

We knew about the bends and we had some knowledge of the Navy diving tables, but a lot of what we were doing was trial and error.

I was still very involved in spearfishing competitions at that time, when I met Ron Church, who was one of the best spearfishermen and he was also a professional underwater photographer. He had a Rollei marine underwater camera system. I had no serious camera at that time, so Ron offered to share his with me. I started going scuba diving with Ron taking underwater still photos. His Rollei marine held a film canister with 12 exposures. We'd dive together and Ron would take the camera and take a picture. Then he'd hand it to me, and he'd start looking for the next picture, and I'd take a picture. We would swap off like that. At the end of the day, we'd have 12 pictures, which was not much, but they were pretty good, as we took time to make each photo count. I still have one of my first ones hanging in our home.

Holding a camera in my hand gradually began to change the way I saw the underwater world.

One day I thought about the spearfishing and I realized if I did well in a competition, I would get a little brass-plated trophy. I'd had fun in the competitions and those little trophies were great, but I thought if I took pictures and started to be known for underwater photography instead of spearfishing, maybe people would start paying me a lot of money for my photos instead of just patting me on the back and handing me a trophy for killing a big fish. That's when I became an environmentalist. I said, "You know what? I think I'm done spearfishing. Underwater photography is the way I'm headed."

From Selling Beer to Selling Scuba Gear

By the mid- to late-1950s there was a growing interest in scuba diving in California. Fueled in part by early episodes of *Sea Hunt*, which first aired in 1958, more and more people were interested in learning to dive. Things started to come together for me to start the Diving Locker.

I had gained a lot of experience owning and running Chuck's Market, a small, full-service grocery. We sold a little bit of everything—meats and fruits and dairy products and such. And we sold a lot of beer and wine. Thank God we sold a lot of beer and wine, because that's where we made most of our profit.

Because my family and I spent so much time at the beach, it seemed practically everyone in our social circle was a diver. The market's sales representative for Gallo wines was Homer Rydell. Homer was in and out of Chuck's Market often, and we became friends. I learned that he was a diver and that his wife Marge dived with Conrad "Connie" Limbaugh at Scripps Institute of Oceanography in La Jolla.

Connie Limbaugh purchased one of the first scuba units ever sold in the United States in 1949 and used it while conducting underwater research as a graduate student at UCLA. Limbaugh went on to become the first "Marine Diving Specialist" at Scripps University in 1953. He was instrumental in developing the first public scuba training certification, founded by Los Angeles County. So, Limbaugh and about eight other divers including Jimmy Stewart, Dr. Wheeler North and Andy Rechnitzer, all experienced divers and most of them graduate students or staff at Scripps Institute of Oceanography, had a contract with the City of San Diego to document conditions on the seafloor in the area where the city was building a sewer outflow. They collected plant and animal specimens, studying them to determine what effects the sewage might have on the environment, and writing reports on their findings. They were well paid for their efforts, and when the contract was finished they had about $5,000 remaining. They wanted to start a retail dive business, so they leased a commercial building in Pacific Beach. Now, these guys were obviously very smart, but none of them had any experience in retail, which is why they reached out to me. I knew about diving and was good at managing a small business—I knew how long it took a check to clear the bank and how to place orders and stock inventory and how to sell practically anything. They made me the manager of the new dive store, which was called the Diving Locker. They continued to do research and stored specimens in a room in back of the retail area. And they invited Ron Church to start a photographic business located inside the Diving Locker. By working our connections within the fledgling diving industry we were able to stock the retail area with inventory and we had just enough money to invest in a Rix air compressor, which at that time was a state-of-the-art piece of equipment for filling scuba tanks.

And that's how the Diving Locker got its start. Our grand opening day was scheduled for June 15, 1959.

Shark Attack

On June 14, 1959, the day before we were scheduled to open the doors of the Diving Locker for the very first time, the first shark attack death happened in La Jolla. I remember that day vividly, but the details of the attack that I'll share here are cobbled together from various news reports I found on the Internet:

The victim's name was Robert Pamperin, age 33. He and his dive buddy, Gerald Lehrer took their girlfriends to the beach at La Jolla cove. The women stayed on the beach while the men went abalone hunting in water about 30 to 40 feet deep not far from shore. The men were using snorkel gear but were not wearing wet suits. According to accounts by Lehrer, the two divers were about 50 feet apart when the shark attack occurred. Lehrer was swimming underwater when he noticed a huge fish swimming over the top of him, disappearing into the kelp. Lehrer surfaced and looked around for Pamperin. He heard him shout for help. That's when he apparently turned and noticed Pamperin with his head unusually high above the surface, without his mask on his face. According to Lehrer, Pamperin quickly disappeared below the surface. Lehrer swam to the spot where he'd seen his dive buddy, took a breath, and dove down. He later reported to authorities that he saw Pamperin in the shark's mouth, his legs not visible. The shark appeared to be twisting from side to side.

Lehrer identified the shark, estimated to be over 20 feet in length, as a great white.

Realizing there was nothing he could do, Lehrer swam toward shore. He was met by William Abitz, who had been standing on a rocky point overlooking the attack site and said he witnessed the attack from shore.

Divers from nearby Scripps Institute of Oceanography were called to the scene to recover Pamperin's body, but it was never found.

Of course I felt bad for the victim and his buddy and their families, but I have to admit that when I heard news of the attack my first thought was, "Now what are our chances? We hadn't even officially opened for business yet and already we were doomed."

Despite the shark attack we decided to go ahead and open the Diving Locker as scheduled. The new store did get a lot of media attention that day—but not the kind anyone would want. As far as the newspapers and TV reports told it, the ocean was a dangerous place and those who were crazy enough to go freediving and scuba diving risked being eaten alive by a shark. We answered a lot of questions—but we sold nothing. The shark attack and the media frenzy that followed made people fearful. It took a while for the fear to subside, but after a while things returned to normal and business improved.

Back When
Everything Was New

I hate the way the word pioneer gets used, but the dictionary defines it as, "one who is first or earliest in any field" and the truth is, when we started the Diving Locker, we had a lot of firsts—especially with new equipment and with scuba training. So I guess you could say we were pioneers.

Even though I'm old, I'm no historian. But I think it's important to tell the story of how scuba training got its start and how Californians were some of its pioneers. Many of my friends and dive buddies made significant contributions to the sport, and I want to recognize their achievements, because without them, I'd never have gotten to enjoy the life I've lived. So with permission from Dr. Alex Brylske, senior editor of *Dive Training* magazine, I'm borrowing an excerpt from a feature article he published, titled, "How Did We Get Here? A Short History of Diver Training." Alex explains how the sport of scuba diving evolved out of freediving—and he does it better than I could:

Understanding the evolution of scuba training in North America is impossible without first exploring the evolution of its predecessor, freediving. That is, diving without the aid of scuba. While freediving certainly took place here on this side of the Atlantic, perhaps the most significant events driving it forward occurred in post-World War I Europe. And while many anonymous free divers no doubt braved the world beneath the waves, it was one intrepid American who brought free diving into public focus. He was a World War I aviator and expatriate named Guy Gilpatric who started diving to catch fish while living on the French Riviera. Aside from a crude pole spear, Gilpatric's gear included only a pair of his flying goggles that he had sealed with putty and paint. He didn't even have a pair of fins. What brought Gilpatric to a role of prominence was not necessarily his prowess but the fact that he wrote about it. As a freelance journalist he published a series of articles about "goggling" in the widely popular Saturday Evening Post magazine, giving folks on this side of the pond their first exposure to what we would later term recreational diving. In 1938, his articles were compiled into what is now an obscure but important book, which some describe as the real catalyst of recreational diving. That book, "The Compleat Goggler," has long been out of print, but you can still find copies for sale occasionally on eBay. By the early 1930s, pioneers like Californians Glen Orr, Jack Prodanovich, and Ben Stone formed the first spearfishing club in the United States — the famous San Diego Bottom Scratchers (which still exists today).

What Gilpatric started, these pioneers refined. The Bottom Scratchers developed improved equipment, refined freediving techniques, and by sharing their knowledge, provided what amounted to the first diver training in America. But the device that was eventually to liberate freedivers from the constraints of their lung capacity was still a few years — and another World War — in the future. This story, too, begins in Europe.

One of Gilpatric's protégés was a young French naval officer who took up free diving as therapy in recovering from a near-fatal auto accident. From our perspective as divers, this was clearly the most significant auto accident in history because the victim was none other than Jacques-Yves Cousteau. Rather than merely spearing fish, though, Cousteau had a passion for filmmaking; and an obvious film subject was the undersea world to which Gilpatric had introduced him. The problem was that filmmakers had to remain underwater longer than spearfishers, and the time limitation imposed by breath-holding just wouldn't work.

Being a naval officer, Cousteau was already familiar with a self-contained diving apparatus developed a decade earlier by another Frenchman named Le Prieur. So, Cousteau went to Paris in the fall of 1942 to meet with Emile Gagnan. A talented engineer whose specialty was valves, Gagnan agreed to help Cousteau. He proposed a valve based on a design he had invented that would convert automobiles from gasoline to natural gas.

Their original design was only marginally successful, and Cousteau almost drowned during a test dive. But after significant retooling, the device was pronounced a success in the summer of 1943. With a simple, safe and reliable breathing apparatus, the stage was set for the creation of the new sport of scuba diving. All that was needed now was a way of training people how to use it. For the next chapter in our story we return to America.

While the actual events are sometimes disputed, most believe that the new "aqualung" was brought to the United States in 1948 by a Navy UDT commander, Doug Fane. The next year, Cousteau sent six units to a friend, Rene Bussoz, who owned a sporting goods store near the UCLA campus. Seeing the potential value of scuba for scientific investigation, a young graduate student, Conrad Limbaugh, convinced his professor to buy two of the units. Soon after, Limbaugh, along with an associate, Andy Rechnitzer, began diving along the Southern California coast.

In 1950 the two enrolled in the Ph.D. program at San Diego's Scripps Institute of Oceanography, and the first scuba training in the United States — the informal tutoring Limbaugh and Rechnitzer did for their colleagues — had begun. The need for more formalized training was soon apparent when in 1952 a student at another California university died in a diving accident.

Alarmed by the death, the Scripps administration asked Limbaugh to create a training course and manual. The result was the first formal scuba training program and textbook in the United States. In 1954, also concerned over the potential hazards of this increasingly popular sport, the Los Angeles County Department of Parks and Recreation sent three representatives — Al Tilman, Bev Morgan, and Ramsey Parks — to San Diego to take Limbaugh's course. This became the first formal scuba instructor program conducted in the United States. Returning to Los Angeles, the trio formed the nation's first recreational scuba training program under the auspices of the Los Angeles Department of Recreation and Parks, a program that still exists today.

In December 1951, two of diving's earliest and most influential enthusiasts, Chuck Blakeslee and Jim Auxier, published the first periodical devoted exclusively to the sport, *Skin Diver* magazine. At first it was geared toward spearfishing and free diving, but soon turned its attention to the increasingly popular activity of scuba. Part of its mission was to enable divers from throughout America to share information. As training was one of the most important areas of concern, *Skin Diver* began a column encouraging instructors to share ideas and techniques on diver training. Written by Neil Hess, "The Instructor's Corner" was an instant success, and any instructor who submitted a course outline for review was listed in the column as a training source.

While California was the center of the country's diving community, events were occurring elsewhere that would have equal influence on diver training. In 1956 the National YMCA formed a committee — headed by National Physical Education Director Bernard Empleton — to publish a textbook based on the then-available resource material related to scuba diving. The committee published the results of its work under the auspices of the Council for National Cooperation in Aquatics (CNCA) — a textbook called "The Science of Skin and Scuba Diving." Although significantly revised, this text is still in print today (retitled "The New Science of Skin and Scuba Diving") and used in some diving programs. In August 1959 the YMCA conducted America's first national instructor training program.

By 1960, Neil Hess felt that diver training should be more organized, and instructor training more controlled than could be achieved through the informal process of his Instructor's Corner column. His idea was to start a national training organization using Los Angeles County's diver training program as a model. For guidance Hess turned to Al Tilman, who headed the Los Angeles program. The two organized an instructor certification course in Houston in 1961 that attracted more than 60 of the top diving educators in America. Initially, Hess planned to call the new group the National Diving Patrol, a tribute to the highly successful National Ski Patrol. But that name had already been taken by another entity, and it was decided to call the fledgling organization the National Association of Underwater Instructors (NAUI). Many participants of that first instructor course would eventually go on to make significant contributions to diving, and a few are still active even today.

Over the next few years a small contingent of divers from the Midwest grew increasingly dissatisfied with the existing diver training infrastructure, contending that it was unresponsive to the needs of inland instructors. In response, Ralph Erickson, an aquatics instructor from Chicago's Loyola University — and graduate of the first NAUI Instructor Institute — along with his friend and diving equipment sales representative, John Cronin, formed the Professional Association of Diving Instructors (PADI) in 1966. In 1973, seeking to establish a more national perspective, PADI moved from Chicago to the Mecca of the American diving scene, Southern California.

There was one other dive specialty shop in the region, the San Diego Diving Supply. Dick Long started his Diving Unlimited shop out in La Mesa about that time, too, so we weren't the only ones.

Scuba training wasn't the only new thing being developed at the time. Wet suits were just starting to make an appearance. Before wet suits, we'd been using a strange combination of "sort of dry" suits. They were supposed to keep the water out, but they leaked. We also tried wearing thick wool sweaters just to keep a little warmth on our bodies.

When neoprene first became available from a company called Rubatex, it came in sheets, and was slick on both sides. Bob and Billy Miestrell and Bev Morgan had started the Dive 'N' Surf dive shop in Redondo Beach, California a few years before we opened the Diving Locker. They were the first ones to make wet suits out of closed-cell neoprene rubber instead of latex-coated canvas. Bev and the Meistrells developed a wet suit that they called the Dive 'N' Surf Thermocline. It later became known as the Body Glove. That suit was the start of the Body Glove wet suit line, which became a huge success and is still successful today.

Bev came to the Diving locker and showed me how to make wet suits and helped us design our wet suit patterns. Bev got us off to a good start; we made wet suits in the back room of the Diving Locker for the next 30 years.

I feel it would have been impossible to start the Diving Locker and have it succeed at that time in history without my friends Connie Limbaugh, Jim Stewart, Andy Rechnitzer, and Wheeler North. Their relationships with the scientific diving community were integral to our success.

At that time we had some of the best divers in the world teaching our scuba classes, which were held in the back room of the Diving Locker. I am grateful for the expertise of all those who taught for the Diving Locker, especially Jimmy Stewart, Wheeler North and Emil Habecker.

Getting By With a
Little Help from My Friends

Over the span of 42 years we trained thousands of divers at the Diving Locker. The first seven years the Diving Locker was at 4825 Cass Street in Pacific Beach, right next to Roger's Automotive and Repair body shop.

There was an old house that was being renovated into a commercial building on Grand Avenue in Pacific Beach and Dr. Wheeler North suggested that was where we should move the store, 1020 Grand Avenue. We loved the idea of moving to a more prominent location, but didn't have the cash for that kind of real estate—$50,000 was a lot of money back then. Dr. North personally bought the property and building and then sold it to me, and my sons Flip and Terry. At the time, I wondered how we'd ever pay off the mortgage, but our many years of hard work paid off. That property turned out to be a great investment.

Over the years I bought back stock from my Scientific Diving Consultants partners, and a couple of them just signed their shares over to me. They were all scientists with other aims in life, but my goal was to make the Diving Locker succeed. Over the next 30 years I ended up the sole owner of the SDC corporation.

Owning the Diving Locker was a rollercoaster ride of highs and lows.

One of the greatest things that happened was having Jacques Cousteau and his team come walking through the door. Cousteau was in town demonstrating the Soucoupe, which was a new type of small submersible. I think he was with Connie and Wheeler, and that's where I met Captain Cousteau for the first time. We had a class going on at the time and I asked him if he'd introduce himself to the class. Jacques Cousteau went in the back room of the Diving Locker, and we introduced him and he welcomed our class of scuba students to his "Silent World."

Later Ron Church became one of the pilots of the Cousteau submersibles.

One of the lowest, saddest times was when we learned of Connie Limbaugh's death. On March 20, 1960 Conrad Limbaugh died when he lost his way in the labyrinth that was the underground river at Port Miou, 20 miles from Marseille, France while filming a type of saltwater fish that reportedly traveled into the freshwater river to rid themselves of parasites. He was 35 years old.

One week later a team of professional cave divers found his body some 350 feet from the entrance to the cave. Limbaugh was buried in a small cemetery overlooking the Mediterranean at Cassis, France. His diving equipment, including his camera gear, was later returned to Scripps.

The scientific and recreational diving communities reacted with shock. I was devastated. He was one of my best friends, and a great guy. Connie was responsible for getting me started in the diving business. I owed him everything.

Not long after his death, Connie's wife Nan gave me one of the greatest gifts I have ever received; she gave me Connie's Rollei marine camera—which was state-of-the-art in still photography at that time— and a Kodak K-100 16-mm movie camera and underwater housing. It seems that even after his death, Conrad Limbaugh was once again my benefactor, providing me with the tools I needed to get a solid start as an underwater photographer and filmmaker.

My passion for underwater photography turned to determination; I was determined to make good use of my friend's posthumous gift. And I also had the support of my friend and mentor, Ron Church, who was instrumental in helping me hone my photography skills.

Once again, I am grateful for all those who played a major role in my success, especially Conrad Limbaugh and Ron Church.

My friend Mary Lynn Price wrote a very detailed biography of Conrad Limbaugh that lists his many accomplishments. To read it, go to scilib.ucsd. edu/sio/biogr/Limbaugh_Biogr.pdf

The Man Who Rode a Whale

Jim Fallon was the first employee at the Diving Locker, and back in the 1960s we were diving all the time. We'd be in the water by 7 a.m. and then we'd get to the Diving Locker and have the doors open by 9 o'clock. And if one of us wanted to go diving during the day, the other guy would cover things at the store.

It was one of those routine "gone diving" days that provided another stroke of good fortune to my career as a professional cameraman. My friend Bill DeCourt and I were on Al Santmyer's boat, the *Duchess*, headed out to La Jolla's Black Rock area, hunting for lobsters. The boat was headed north of La Jolla when we spotted something big at the surface. It was a whale. In San Diego, it was pretty common to see grey whales close to shore, especially during the winter months. But this one was different; it was just staying on the surface, not moving. I wanted to get a closer look, so I talked our dive group into stopping the boat so I could get in the water with the whale. Al gave the okay to enter, and Bill and I hit the water like we'd been shot out of a cannon. We had my K-100 16-mm movie camera and the Rollei marine still camera. As we approached the whale it was suddenly apparent why it wasn't moving—it was entangled in a giant gill net. The weight of the net was dragging the whale down; it was at a 45-degree angle to the surface and we could see that it was struggling to surface for air, the net cutting into its flukes, rendering them useless. The whale was in danger of drowning.

Bill and I started freeing the whale, filming as we worked. The whale didn't struggle, but just let us do our thing. I think that's part of what motivated me to climb on its back. It was so calm. I just climbed on its back and sat there, smiling.

And Bill got the photos to prove it.

You have to remember that in those days people thought of whales as killer beasts instead of the gentle giants we now know them to be. No one had ever gotten close to one in the water, for fear that they'd be killed. And I'd just become the first person ever known to ride on a whale.

It didn't occur to me at the time that sitting on the whale, which we later identified as a Bryde's fin whale, would be such a big deal. But the *San Diego Union-Tribune* newspaper ran a photo of me atop the whale and the photo ended up in newspapers nationwide and within a few weeks I had interviews from newspapers around the world. All the sudden I became known as "the man who rode a whale." As far as the media was concerned, I was now considered a whale expert—which ironically proved to be a pivotal step in my becoming a professional photographer.

Photo courtesy of the *San Diego Union-Tribune.*

On Glamour and *Geographic*

Ask anyone who's made a successful career out of doing something they truly love, and they'll probably tell you that the road to their success wasn't all paved and glamorous.

Not all the diving we did was the "fun" kind. In fact, we were fortunate that through our connections at Scripps we started getting some commercial diving work—some important "paycheck" jobs. The work was far from glamorous, like diving on pipelines, inspecting them for leaks and filming our findings. We'd start at the bottom in 200 feet of water and follow the pipeline all the way to shore. We worked cleaning the intakes of the power plant in the south bay. That kind of stuff. There was nothing sexy about it, but it paid the bills.

Every now and then a cool gig came along. For instance, I worked with Jon Lindbergh, who was testing a one-man submarine. It had no motor, operating instead on some kind of hydraulic ebb and flow movement through the water. I did some filming for him.

Then one day while I was working at the Diving Locker I got a call from Bates Littlehales, a staff photographer at *National Geographic* magazine. I thought to myself, why are they calling me? That's when Bates explained that he and Louie Martin, the chief underwater photographer at *Geographic*, were interested in filming grey whales. He said they'd seen a newspaper report of me riding a whale and thought I might be able to help them. Recognizing that this was, in fact, *National Geographic* on the phone, I didn't spend a whole lot of time reminding them that at the time I "rode" the whale, it happened to be weighed down by a massive gill net and was nearly drowned. I tried to play it cool. I let Bates know that while I was far from a whale expert, I had tried to film grey whales on several occasions, with no measurable results. I added that I knew it was challenging work and said yes of course I would indeed be interested in working with *National Geographic.* I'd help out any way I could.

Bates Littlehales met me in San Diego and we spent about a month pursuing migrating grey whales. We spent most of that time just hanging out, waiting for the chance to get in the water with the whales. But in the process Bates and I became really close friends. We did end up going to Baja with a hot air balloon to take topside pictures of the grey whales, but our efforts at getting underwater images were pretty much a bust.

Bates mentioned that one of his next big assignments would take him to Turkey to film an archeological operation with Dr. George Bass. He asked me if I would like to come along as his assistant. I said, great. I mean, what more could you wish for than a chance to work with a photographer at *National Geographic?*

Time went on, and in the spring, Bates called me and said he had a job to do in the Bahamas, but we were still on for the early fall assignment in Turkey. He explained that I'd need to meet him in Washington D.C. for a few days before we left for Turkey. Fine by me. I was thrilled to have the opportunity.

Not long before we were scheduled to make the trip, I got another call from Bates. He said, "Chuck, I'm sorry, but we have a problem. I burst an eardrum during the Bahamas assignment. I won't be able to go to Turkey to do the George Bass deep-water wreck job. *National Geographic* still wants the story. Would you be willing to go shoot it on your own?"

I nearly fell out of my chair. I remember I had to take several deep breaths before I could make words come out of my mouth—and when they finally did, I said something like, "Of course, Bates. I'll do it. I'm sorry to hear about your burst eardrum, but I'm happy to help out. Just let me know what I need to do." But you know what? What I was thinking sounded more like, "This could be my big chance, but wow, I'm getting into something that's way over my head. I'd better not screw this up."

By this point I'd been putting a lot of effort into improving my photography skills, and I was taking full advantage of the mentoring Ron Church so generously provided. But I had been shooting with a Bronica, a camera that has a "two and a quarter" format. I had no experience with a 35-mm camera. I flew to D.C. for three days of indoctrination at *National Geographic*'s headquarters. They handed me two 35-mm Nikons and a bunch of film, and instructed me to go out on the streets and shoot. I spent the next two days looking through a viewfinder, taking black and white photos. The film was processed each night and the next day we talked about the results and how to improve. I learned this is the way they did it at *Geographic*. It doesn't matter how you think you want to do it, you always do it the *Geographic* way. The nice thing was that everyone was helpful, and very encouraging. They realized that I was already into something I hadn't done before, and that I was eager to learn. Somehow I managed to pull it off—so off I went. They gave me a couple booklets, an instruction manual and a funky metal Oceanic housing for a Leica camera with no wide-angle lenses. They gave me a whole bunch of brand new equipment: two of the new Calypso cameras with 35-mm lenses, and some strobes that were just coming out that were developed for *Geographic* by Harold Edgerton, and a camera bag full of Nikon camera bodies and lenses. The next thing I knew, I was on a plane for Turkey. On a photo assignment for *National Geographic* magazine.

I was in Turkey for more than a month, living on Yassida Island off the port of Bodrum. I made a lot of friends, shot hundreds of photos, and had one helluva good time. Diving with George Bass and archeology students and professors from the University of Pennsylvania was really interesting. It was a little deeper diving than most of them were used to, though. The wreck sat at 130 feet.

I had been diving a lot deeper with Scripps in California's cold dirty water, and here we were at 130 feet in clear, fairly warm water; I thought it was a piece of cake. We did have an air-filled decompression chamber that was lowered and raised from a pulley system on the beach. Theoretically, we'd go into the two-person chamber at 20 feet and make a safety stop, and then they'd raise it up to ten feet for another safety stop, and when time was up we could go to the boat. It was more comfortable than hanging in the water, but the logistics weren't great so we weren't able to use the chamber all the time.

When the chamber wasn't operational we spent a lot of time doing deco stops hanging onto a weighted line off the back of the boat. We tied a bucket to the line at 15 feet and on the way down to do our dive I'd usually put a book and an apple or carrot inside the bucket for later, so I'd have something to read and snack on during my deco stop. The other divers thought I was a little nuts; they didn't understand how I could be so casual about diving deep and having to decompress. I was just used to it, is all.

The *National Geographic* issue with the article on Turkey came out in 1967, and after that I was offered more opportunities to dive with their staff photographers, including Bates. I guess that means I hadn't screwed up.

One of the jobs Bates and I worked on together was on the National Wildlife Refuge in Cabeza Prieta range in southern Arizona. Our assignment was to film gila monsters. Neither one of us knew the first thing about gila monsters, but I did learn they are poisonous. We had a truck and camper that we operated from for about a week.

I flew into town and met Bates at a restaurant near the airport. After he asked how my flight was, he said, "Hey, you want a drink?"

I said, "Sure. I'll have a gin and tonic."

Camera Man

He said, "Wait, you can't put tonic in a good gin. You'll ruin it." From then on, when I did have a drink, which is seldom, I always ordered gin on the rocks.

Bates did the provisioning for our trip, which meant that for some meals were thick steaks and a bottle of Chianti, and for others we had corned beef hash and canned peaches. It was definitely a "good ol' boys" kind of adventure.

We filmed at night, because theoretically, it's better to film gila monsters at night. I'm not sure if that's actually true or not, but it's what we did. Anyway, we got the job done. And we filmed a lot of rattlesnakes, too.

Another assignment I did with Bates had us traveling to Auke Bay, Alaska, to film Alaskan king crabs. During mating, the crabs are said to aggregate in big mounds. We were wearing wet suits, and I'll never forget the painful feeling of bitter cold I felt when we made that first dive. And we got nothing for it. No king crabs.

We moved to Kodiak Island to continue our search for mating king crabs. Bates said we'd have better luck there. We suited up and walked through the snow into the freezing water. If there was a gigantic mound of mating king crabs I doubt we'd have seen it. The visibility was zero.

This just proves that just because it's *National Geographic* doesn't mean things are going to go your way. We got nothing. But at least we didn't freeze to death or get eaten by a giant grizzly bear.

Patagonian Traveling Circus

Another assignment took me to Argentina, working on an article with Bill Curtsinger. The story was based on Dr. Roger Payne's research on southern right whales. Payne and his family were living in a remote encampment atop a cliff on Patagonia's rugged Peninsula Valdes.

The adventure started the minute we arrived in Buenos Aires and learned that our cameras and dive equipment were hung up in customs. That was the bad news. The good news was that we got rooms at the Belvedere Palace hotel while we were waiting for the paperwork to get sorted out. The Belvedere was a pretty fancy hotel, especially for a beach bum like me.

It took about a week for us to get our gear through customs. We traded the posh Belvedere for a couple Fiats—the smallest cars I'd ever seen in my life. They looked like clown cars to start with, and their looks did not improve once we'd packed the cars with dive equipment, cameras, camping gear, a small Zodiac rubber boat and a compressor. We were a traveling circus, for sure. And standing over six feet tall, I was no small clown.

Photographer Andy Pruna joined us. He was on assignment for the New York Zoo Biological Society. Cuban-born, Andy's fluent Spanish proved to be a big plus as we made our way to Puerto Madryn. And he was good company. We became fast friends.

Things were going smoothly as we reached Bahia Blanca, the first stop on our three-day trip south. The two-lane highways were paved, and we were making good time. That all changed quickly enough. As we left Bahia Blanca the two-lane paved highway gave way to a one-lane rock pile. Okay, maybe not a rock pile, but the coarse gravel proved to be hell on our little Fiats. Over the next two days we had about 10 flat tires.

I'm not exaggerating. We had to stop and buy extra tires—and a few extra windshields, too—and strap them on top of the cars. It seemed every truck that passed us sent a rock flying into a windshield, and every attempt to avoid a pothole flattened a tire. It got to the point where there wasn't anything funny about traveling Patagonia by clown car, but we kept heading south and finally ended up on Peninsula Valdes.

We met Roger and his family at their beach encampment and we set up our crappy little tent next to them on the cliff. Despite the fact that we were road weary, sleep didn't come easily. On our way in we'd seen a hotel, so the next day we ditched our tent and set up camp at the Puerto Piramides Hotel.

We filmed Roger with the southern right whales at Gulfo San Jose and Gulfo Nuevo. It was strange, the way the whales seemed to appear and then just disappear. At times there'd be females with calves all over the place, and all the sudden they'd be gone. We asked Roger about it, but he didn't have a definite answer. He theorized that they left the bay for a couple days at a time to feed, and then returned. It didn't seem to matter how many "whale experts" were gathered around, and what our research or filming goals were; the whales came and went as they pleased.

Each morning, the hotel's cook would pack us a lunch of grilled lamb sandwiches on fresh-baked bread—and at the bottom of our lunch basket we'd usually find a bottle of red wine. At lunchtime we'd pull our little Zodiac inflatable close to shore, devour our sandwiches and wash them down with a nice Argentine Malbec. Times like these are what make the hardships of remote travel worthwhile. Except for that one afternoon when we fell asleep after lunch and a swell came up and washed the Zodiac onto the rocks. We nearly capsized.

Thankfully, our film shoot proved to be a success. Working with someone like Bill Curtsinger was a real pleasure. He is a total pro. We worked hard, but we had a lot of good times, too. That trip was a good indoctrination into filming whales in the real world.

Closer to Home

In between the assignments working with the photographers at *National Geographic*, I was making other deals, still working to get my foot in the door as a cameraman or still photographer. And of course, I stayed plenty busy working at the Diving Locker when I was back in San Diego between assignments.

One of the main reasons I had the ability to be gone on film jobs for long stretches of time is that we had a great team of employees at the Diving Locker over the years. They were a loyal, hardworking bunch—too many to mention here—but one that stands out is Gordy Heck. He started at the Diving Locker when he was 16 years old. Gordy became the store manager and worked for the Diving Locker for 25 years.

Because of the Diving Locker's close ties with Scripps I enjoyed many opportunities to dive with their researchers on various projects. I had a couple scuba certification cards issued by Scripps. One was good for a 130-foot rating and the other was for a 200-foot rating, which you could get after making five dives to that depth with a Scripps instructor.

One of the Scripps expeditions I made was to Mexico's Guadalupe Island with Dr. Carl Hubbs. He was a renowned ichthyologist whose amassed a large body of research. He was one of the first scientists to observe changes in fish population patterns depending on the fluctuation in temperatures in the Pacific Ocean—that was back before the buzzwords "climate change" had ever been uttered.

Another interesting tidbit: Guadalupe Island is now known as "the place" where divers can go for guaranteed great white shark encounters. I can't even tell you how many dives we made off

Guadalupe back then—including collecting fish specimens and once, we even captured an elephant seal for the San Diego Zoo—and we never noticed any great whites.

Younger readers probably just cringed at reading, "captured an elephant seal for the San Diego Zoo." All I can say is that times were different then. The ocean was a different place. Back then it seemed like the ocean was a limitless resource. I was just a young freelancer, doing anything that would promote more diving for the Diving Locker and help put some coins in my pocket. I also filmed for SeaWorld when they were making live fish collections off Cabo San Lucas and around the Socorro Island group. We did a lot of things that today would be deemed politically incorrect. Many of the things I did back then are things I wouldn't do today.

A Stowaway on a Submarine

Not all of my work involved filming marine animals. Over the years I had several opportunities to film submarines, which in some often proved just as challenging as filming finicky whales.

One show was with a local television station, Channel 8. Bob Dale had a daytime show, and once did a piece on submarines. Bob arranged for us to film on a submarine operating out of Ballast Point. His TV camera crew was filming topside and I was there to film the underwater segment.

Up near the bow of the submarine there was a small hatch used for loading torpedoes. They wanted footage of the submarine's conning tower going up and down. The plan was for me to stuff myself in the small space in order to get the shot. We all figured there'd be no way the Navy would let me ride on the outside of a submarine while it was underway, but the captain was a nice guy. He probably put his career on the line, letting a civilian filmmaker do such a thing, but he took that old diesel submarine out into the bay with me, in full scuba gear, wedged into the torpedo bay hatch like a stowaway. But that's exactly what we did. I had a 16-mm camera and got shots of the deck and the conning tower going underwater. The dive was just sort of a skim dive, down and up. I filmed the whole time. They were all pretty excited when the submarine surfaced and they found me still wedged in place. It's still hard to believe we got to do something like that with a Navy submarine.

I also worked with Lockheed's deep submersible, primarily filming their test dives during a time when Lockheed was seeking to get Navy approval for its Deep Quest submersible. Once they got the okay from the Navy, everyone involved got an award recognizing them for being in the submarine. Except me. My certificate said I was filming outside the submarine, at 100 feet.

Along for the Ride

My friend Dr. Andreas "Andy" Rechnitzer was a former Scripps researcher who in 1960 was part of a team that made a record 35,800-foot dive to the bottom of Guam's Marianas Trench in the bathyscaph *Trieste*. For their roles in the *Trieste* Project, Andy and his colleagues were awarded the Presidential Distinguished Citizen Service Award from President Eisenhower.

Andy was a regular guy, but he traveled in some prestigious circles. His friend Pablo Romero Bush was the head of Mexico's Water Sports and Exploration Club called, CEDAM (Club de Exploraciones y Deportes Acuaticos de Mexico). The group had found the wreck of the *Matanceros*, which crashed into the reef near Akumal on February 22, 1741. The group wanted to protect the wreck site and have it designated as a marine archeological preserve and they were enlisting the support of Rechnitzer and other prominent figures, including astronaut Scott Carpenter, automobile designer Carroll Shelby and explorer and filmmaker Peter Gimble. Shelby owned a twin-engine DC-3 airplane and Bush persuaded him to use it to bring a group of VIPs to Cozumel so he could show them the beautiful diving and enlist their help in supporting his goal of a marine park that would protect, among other sites, the wreck of the *Matanceros*. I was invited along for the ride, both as a cameraman and scuba instructor. My role would be to film the diving, and also look after Scott Carpenter's wife Rene, who wasn't really a diver.

So, we flew to Cozumel in a private plane and when we arrived we were escorted to a beautiful beachfront home (which later got destroyed by a hurricane). Sometime during the cocktail party that first night, Carroll Shelby jumped off the sea wall into the sand and sprained his ankle. We had a dive scheduled the next morning and he could hardly walk. The divemaster learned about Carroll's injury, so he showed up with a cane, which none of us could figure out. How was a walking cane going to help a scuba diver? Well, the divemaster helped Carroll put one fin on, and when the two of them got in the water the divemaster looped the hook of the cane onto Carroll Shelby's arm and towed him along the reef. It looked a little crazy, but it was genius.

The owner of the house was a wealthy businessman, Eduardo Velazquez, who owned Mexico's biggest Ford auto parts dealerships. He'd just given his two sons a brand new Bronco, one of the first Ford SUVs. There was a lot of drinking going on and those two teenagers wrecked the brand new Ford. They figured they were in for a lot of trouble if their father found out, so they drove it into a sinkhole, a cenote. Somehow they arranged to have an identical Bronco brought in from Mexico City. They never told their father they wrecked that first car.

We all had quite a week in Cozumel. I got to know Scott Carpenter, and I enjoyed helping his wife feel more comfortable about scuba diving. After the trip she wrote about the experience in her Washington, DC newspaper column.

As we left Cozumel one of the DC-3's engines caught fire and we were forced to make an emergency landing in Merida. Carroll Shelby bought us all tickets to fly back home.

Andy and Pablo Bush had put the whole adventure together. It might have been an unconventional way to promote a conservation effort, but the wreck of the *Matancero* has indeed been preserved. In fact, Pablo Bush Romero has proven instrumental in protecting the cenotes along the Yucatan Peninsula. He's done a great job of making people aware of the value of Mexico's underwater resources.

A Close One

The work that Bill Curtsinger and I had done filming right whales in the waters off Punta Valdes, Argentina had given us credibility as whale filmmakers. Our next *National Geographic* assignment took us to Maui, Hawaii, to film humpback whales. The humpback whales off Maui had become a hot item, and all the scientists were jumping over each other trying to get their foot in the door and become established there.

The Pioneer Hotel in Lahaina was near the docks and the old hotel became the de facto headquarters for most whale film groups. Each morning there would be photographers sitting around having Kona coffee and coconut pancakes—and telling lies. They'd say they had just seen the whales off of Lanai, or they'd say, they're really down south towards the other end of the island. Everybody had a different story.

It was interesting. Bill and I were some the first of the real underwater whale photographers in Maui. Bill was in love with his little 12-foot Zodiac inflatable boat. We'd hauled that boat all over the place from one assignment to the next, and now it was in Hawaii. That was our boat in the channel between Maui and Lanai as we endeavored to photograph humpback whales. It was tough in those days. There weren't as many whales as today, and the whales were very spooky. They were not used to boats following them and definitely not used to people in the water.

Our equipment was really basic. We didn't have the Nikon 35-mm Ocean Eye housings but we were starting to use some wide-angle lenses. One of the first advances was the 21-mm Yashica lens adapted for the Nikonos cameras.

One day when we were working off the coast of Lanai, we found a whale that we thought looked sick. We followed it for quite a while, hoping it would stop. Finally it stopped, and as we started to enter the water a large tiger shark made a pass at our white outboard motor. This tiger shark was longer than our 12-foot boat. The whale started moving again, which was fine by us—as getting in the water to photograph the whale had suddenly lost its appeal. Bill had been bitten on the shoulder by a grey reef shark when he was on a job in the Phoenix Islands, so he was a little reluctant to get in the water.

When the whale stopped a few hours later we figured the shark would not have followed us. When we were filming our routine would be to both get in the water to shoot. One person would hold on to the rope, so the boat wouldn't drift away, leaving the other person free to swim to the whale. We'd alternate, taking turns filming and boat-sitting.

It was Bill's turn to film. We had followed this whale for a while and we finally had a great opportunity to get close. I said, "Okay Bill, let's go for it." He hesitated, so I said, "Bill, we've come a long way and I doubt the tiger shark would have followed the whale all this time. You can stay with the boat. I'll just jump in and see if I can get a shot."

Bill nodded. He stayed in the boat while I jumped in the water with my camera and started swimming towards the whale. Before I could get in position to get close enough to take photographs, the whale moved off again, so I started swimming back to the boat. Just as I got to the boat and started to hand my cameras up to Bill, he screamed, "Watch out!" Bill grabbed me, and as he did, I knew what was happening. I felt the water moving next to me as the tiger shark brushed past my legs. Bill practically ripped my arms off as he helped haul me back into our little rubber boat. That was a close one.

We decided that this wasn't our whale. This wasn't our day. We headed back to shore.

As it turns out, that was the last time Bill Curstinger and I worked together on a *National Geographic* shoot. Bill's a great guy—a very dedicated professional shooter. It was my pleasure to work with him, and to learn from him.

In Deep With David Doubilet

David Doubilet made a name for himself as one of *National Geographic*'s underwater photographers who specialized in fish portraits. Simply put, David is one of the best in the business. We first dived together in the Red Sea in the early 1970s when David was working on a story about Dr. Eugenie Clark.

Later we spent about three weeks diving off British Columbia. The water was cold and we were still using quarter-inch wet suits. We dived Port Hardy and Powell River and especially Race Rocks. What I love about David is that he's his own man. He's the kind of guy who marches to the beat of his own drum—except the drumming doesn't start until around noon. I'm more of a morning person, so it seems like a lot of my time spent working with David involved sitting around waiting for him to wake up. David's schedule worked just fine for diving Race Rocks, though, since the tides weren't usually favorable for diving until around noon, anyway.

One of my most interesting assignments working with David was off Maui, filming the local black coral diver. Black coral jewelry had become an important part of the tourist trade in Hawaii, and the divers had to go deep—180 to 225 feet deep—to harvest it.

David and I were good deep diving buddies by this time and knew we could count on each other in an emergency, which is a good thing, because tt was pretty exciting diving in the channel between Maui and Lanai. The coral divers are really special. They were diving deep and long and smoking weed all the time. Most of them had been bent at least once. Often I don't think they knew if they were bent or not because they were so high.

The funny thing was, they worried that we were too casual about doing our deep dives and our own decompression schedules, so one day they assigned us a student from the University of Hawaii that was there studying the black coral. He was supposed to watch out for us. So, we made our dive, another 200-footer, and after we returned to the surface everyone was sitting around and the black coral divers were all smoking. And our helper? Well he was looking sort of funny. One of the black coral divers says to the assistant diver, "I think you bent, Braddah."

He replied, "No, I'm okay. I'm fine. I just had a late night last night, is all."

One of the "field tests" used to determine if a diver might be bent is to have them urinate. This guy couldn't pee. All the sudden our "babysitter" was the one on emergency oxygen and the boat was headed back to the beach. We never found out if he'd actually suffered a bends hit or if he just had a hangover from too much partying the night before.

While in Maui we also made some dives with the black coral company's submersible. Ricky Grigg, a famous surfer, was the submersible pilot. We did some memorable deep dive photos off the sheer wall along the back side of Molokini Crater.

When our assignment was finished, the "wrap party" with the coral divers and their friends was epic. I'm glad the bill for that one went on David's expense report and not mine.

Shooting Up a Storm

One of my Diving Locker partners and a dear friend, Wheeler North had contacts everywhere. His friend Alan Minor was a Hollywood director/producer. Wheeler set me up to meet with Alan. This was my first chance to be involved with a real film producer at Warner Brothers.

The film he was working on was called *Chubasco*, which is a Spanish word for storm. The film was set on a large tuna fishing boat by the same name, and the story was a drama based on the boat owner's family.

I met Alan in San Diego harbor, where the boat was docked. Alan explained that the film would be shot in Panavision, which was a 70-mm format. I barely knew what Panavision was, but I knew it meant this was a bigtime Hollywood project. He took me to look at the camera housing, which was the first underwater housing built for a major Hollywood film. The housing was massive, about the size of a steamer trunk set on end. I was just starting to ask a lot of questions about the camera and housing when Alan got a phone call. Before he excused himself to take the call he pointed to a young man standing nearby and said, "This guy, he's going to be your assistant. He'll help you."

My first thought was that maybe I got the job. My second thought was, "How do I work this giant thing," so I asked the guy, "What do you know about this camera system?"

"Everything," he replied.

"Great," I said. "Once we get this thing in the water, you show me where the camera trigger is and we'll be a great team for this movie."

That's the way my filming big Hollywood movies started. The first scenes I filmed were from the surface, and included various takes of the boat cruising past. Some were of the boat entering and leaving the harbor; others were of the boat out in open water. That kind of thing.

The giant housing was buoyant in the water. It had a series of adjustable lead weights attached to it, so it was pretty easy to get the housing to float at or just below the surface, but because of its size it proved difficult to push around. On the first day of filming I spent a few hours at the surface with the huge Panavision system. One of the boat crew was assigned to swim behind me to protect me (or at least the camera) making sure the boat knew where we were to keep us from being run over. The tuna boat captain was a very experienced skipper; we weren't in any danger.

The degree of difficulty ratcheted up a notch or two on the next scene, when we added blue sharks.

In *Chubasco*, a young man chooses a life of hard labor, working aboard a tuna fishing boat when he falls in love with the boat captain's daughter. He and the captain clash over this budding romance. In one action-packed scene they're pulling in the tuna nets, which are straining with the weight of the catch—which includes a lot of blue sharks. As the tension between the two men builds, a big metal pulley breaks loose from the rigging and hits the young man, knocking him overboard into the net full of sharks. Despite his dislike for the young man the captain risks his life, jumping into the net full of sharks to save him.

The big metal pulley was actually made of Styrofoam. But the sharks were real. One of my first takes was to film a stuntman as he gets knocked into the water. He's supposed to flail around in the water with the tunas and sharks as if he's drowning, and then swim to the net and cling to it while fighting off the frenzied sharks.

The stunt man gives a damn fine performance, hitting the water and flailing like crazy. It looks like he's really drowning. I'm filming away, getting really good stuff, when it occurs to me that the stuntman isn't acting. He's really drowning. I yelled up to the boat, "Hey, this is real. He's drowning." All the sudden I'm holding the stuntman up by his shirt collar with one hand, while trying to balance the giant camera housing in the other. I managed to swim him over to the fishing net, which we'd rigged close to the boat. I told him to hang on while some other film crew brought a little skiff over and got him out of the water.

Later when we were all back on the tuna boat, I asked the stuntman, "What the hell went wrong?"

His response stunned me. "I can't swim," he confessed.

I couldn't believe it, asking, "Why in the world did you agree to do the stunt? Are you crazy?"

"I really needed this job," he said. "I thought it wouldn't be a big thing, that I could at least swim enough to make it to the net and hang on—long enough for us to get the shot—but I just started sinking. I really can't swim."

This was my first exposure to some of the stuntmen of Hollywood. Some were highly skilled guys who were wonderful to work with, and a few turned out to be real clowns that somehow got let onto movie sets by mistake.

Of course, this was also my first time filming a major motion picture. A lot of crazy stuff happens on a movie set. But I enjoyed the work. The film *Chubasco* was released by Warner Brothers in 1968 starring Christopher Jones, Susan Strasberg and Richard Egan.

Al Giddings

You'll see the name Al Giddings all over this book, as he is the man most responsible for my film career. He's also one of my very best friends.

When we first met back in the early 1960s Al and I shared a passion for freediving and spearfishing. Al was a really good spearfisherman. Most of the early underwater photographers started out as hunters who reached a point where they said, well, what's next? The next thing was underwater photography. As I mentioned earlier in the book, some friends of mine at the Diving Locker had just started the San Diego Underwater Photographic Society and we were planning a film festival at the Civic auditorium. Al had recently made a promotional film for US Divers scuba equipment Company, a 16-mm film called *The Painted Reefs of Honduras.* I invited Al to show his film, and it was a big success. While on stage at the festival, Al thanked the audience for their support—and then he told the crowd that I would soon be traveling to Cozumel with him to make a film. After the festival, Al pulled me aside, saying, "I'm serious, Chuck. I'm doing another promo film for US Divers. This one will be shot in Cozumel and it'll be called *Twilight Reef.* Come with me. Let's make this film together."

I thanked him for the offer, explaining that I had my dive business to run and that there was no way I could afford to be away from the dive shop.

Al was undaunted. I remember him saying, "I'll phone you when I get back to San Francisco."

Sure enough, about a week later I got a call from Al Giddings. Gloria was there when I got the call, and she's the one who convinced me to go. She kept repeating, "I think you need to do this. It sounds like a chance you shouldn't pass up." That's how I ended up in Cozumel, filming Twilight Reef with Al Giddings.

We did some incredible dives. Black coral was the big thing in those days and the large corals down 200-feet deep along the wall on Palancar reef were gigantic—several were the size of a Christmas tree. This was one of my first diving expeditions outside of Baja, so I was thrilled.

Together we shot a nice little film and that trip cemented a forever friendship. When we were done, Al thanked me for joining him and said he'd like to work with me again. I remember saying something like, "Al it's been a pleasure, and I'd be glad to work with you, any time. In the meantime I'll have to go home for a while, sell a bunch of dive gear and keep making wet suits."

From then on, Al and I became very close friends and we filmed all over the world. I was his main cinematographer, and backed him up any way I could. I always had a special relationship with Al. He understood that I had things that I wanted to do, besides making underwater films. The diving business was mostly my dependable livelihood.

Al would work hard to put together the ideas for a film and get the backing. When it was set up, he'd call me saying, "Chuck, we're going to make a film." I didn't need a whole lot of details. I'd go to the airport, pick up my ticket and be off to a filming location somewhere in the world. It didn't matter where we went. Al would make sure that I always had the best accommodations. I became known as Al's right-hand man when it came to working with the crew. If they didn't understand the work schedule or the financials or whatever, I worked it out with them. It was important the crew worked as a solid team, understanding exactly what Al expected of them in order to get the job done—no matter what. I handled a lot of that stuff so that Al could concentrate on other things.

Some people have a mistaken idea of what it's like to work on a film crew, like it's a glamorous, high-paying gig. The crew was not highly paid in those days. We worked long hours and there'd be times when the crew was tired and hungry and they'd start growing impatient. Al would be saying, "Come on, we got to get one more shot. It doesn't matter how many times we've done it. Let's go again." He was a perfectionist and it had to be done his way. So I tried reverse psychology on him. I would say, "Yeah, you're right Al. We might not have it yet. We'd better do it again." Most times Al would say, "Wait a minute," and then he would say, "No. I think we have it. Let's go ahead and quit for the day."

If I thought we should film a repeat scene, or I didn't think my shot was what I wanted for my part of the scene I'd say, "Al, I think that's good enough. I think we got it," and he'd say, "No, not so fast. Let's shoot this again." I don't know if he ever caught on to me (although now, my secret is out). However we did it, we've worked well together all these years. And it's been a whole lot of fun.

Al Giddings is another story and probably Al should have been the one to write this book. I love him. He's a tough guy, but he's also a hard worker. He became hugely successful because he always worked harder than anyone else. He might not be the greatest artist in the business, but he has the vision and the drive for achieving great success. He's the guy who would get the best results under the toughest conditions. Every time.

Fighting Off a Dead Shark

In 1975 I had the opportunity to work with Al Giddings in Bonaire on a film called *Sharks' Treasure*. Cornel Wilde was the producer and director. He was also the star. It wasn't Cornel's first film in which he'd had multiple roles, both in front of and behind the camera, as he'd also produced, directed and starred in a film called *The Naked Prey*. The film came out in 1965. Set in the South African lowlands, it was a wilderness survival story loosely based on the life of explorer John Colter, who was hunted by Blackfoot Indians on the prairies of Wyoming in 1809. Cornell was about 60 at the time that film was shot. He was in excellent condition, but imagined himself to be in the shape of a 21-year old.

The storyline for *Sharks' Treasure* was corny—a bunch of ex-cons trying to take over a treasure-hunting expedition. But remember, these were the early days of underwater filmmaking.

Anyway, a film that had to do with the underwater world had to have sharks. Lots of sharks. One scene called for Cornel, one of the treasure hunters, to be working from inside a cage to protect himself from sharks, when a big shark goes berserk and starts attacking the cage. Cornel uses part of a thick broomstick to "fight off" the shark.

The sharks used for the film were caught at night for use in the next day's filming. Unfortunately, many of the sharks didn't live to have a starring role in the film. They'd die during the night.

In Cornel's big shark-fight scent, the shark we filmed was unfortunately dead. We held the shark up and Cornel, being very strong, had the shark sort of stuck on the end of the stick in its jaws. The shark was nearly six feet long, but Cornell was able to convincingly move it around like it was fighting the stick in its mouth. We avoided shooting too close, and the scene actually worked, despite the fact that the "attack shark" was quite dead at the time that scene was filmed.

When we went to Australia's Coral Sea to film grey reef sharks, thoracic surgeon Dr. Stan Berman, was hired to be on set during filming, in case of an actual shark incident. Stan had his own 8-mm movie camera for shooting home movies. We'd thrown a lot of bait in the water, attracting many sharks. Stan attempted to be inconspicuous about doing his own filming, but Cornel spotted him and was furious. He thought it careless of Stan to be distracted, taking his own photos instead of standing by, ready to help one of us survive a shark bite.

Sharks' Treasure had a pretty realistic set, including cannons, replica coins, jewelry and artifacts. After the film shoot wrapped the crew was given coins to take home as souvenirs. I had some of them in ashtray at my beach house, and during a party one evening someone stole all those replica coins. I wish I had been there when they tried to sell them.

Just as a side story, around this time two of the leading underwater cinematographers were Lamar Boren and Jordan Klein. Lamar Boren was a very quiet person living in La Jolla, California and designing and building his camera housings. Jordan Klein was based out of Miami Florida. Jordan had developed Mako Housings that were the first commercial professional camera housings developed in United States.

Lamar made housings for 70-mm, and then 35-mm cameras used in movie production and the *Sea Hunt* television series He was a real character. The Diving Locker could not sell Lamar a wet suit. He did most of the filming for *Sea Hunt* wearing just his swim trunks. He was big man, probably weighing 250-plus pounds, so he did have a fair amount of natural insulation, but still. He'd jump in the water and be just fine when everyone else was complaining about Catalina Island's cold water temperatures.

I thought maybe I might somehow gain entry into the film business through working with Lamar. I had just finished shooting *Shark Treasure* with Al Giddings and Lamar was filming the James Bond thriller, *Thunderball.* I phoned Lamar and let him know I was willing to work for him as an intern to learn the business. I told Lamar, "I'll do anything. I'll carry your swim trunks. I'll load cameras. I'm eager to work with you." He very politely said, "Chuck, that's great. I appreciate your enthusiasm. I'll give you a call."

I followed up with another phone call a few weeks later, but got nowhere. Lamar said he was too busy to talk right then, but that he'd be in touch soon.

I never heard back. We saw each other a few times over the years, but he was just not interested in anyone else getting into the underwater film business as a cinematographer. I don't really blame him. He had the whole field pretty much to himself, and he was really good at what he did, whether it was in fabricating camera housings, or filming.

Adventures on the *Andrea Doria*

Without a doubt, the Italian cruise liner *Andrea Doria* is among the world's most challenging wreck dives. On July 25, 1956 after colliding with another liner, the *Stockholm*, the *Doria* sank in 250 feet of water 160 miles off the coast of New York. The deep depth, cold, dark water and strong currents make for difficult diving. In fact, it's known as the "Mount Everest" of wreck diving. More than a dozen divers have lost their lives on the *Doria*.

In 1968 I had the opportunity to join Al Giddings and Jack McKenney on an expedition to dive the *Doria* as part of a filming and treasure-recovery effort spearheaded by Nick Zinkowski and Alan Krasberg. Zinkowski, a hardhat diver, was the chief diving officer. Krasberg, a physicist at Westinghouse, was a pioneer in closed-circuit mixed gas deep diving.

We had some interesting dives on the *Andrea Doria*. It was 170 feet to the deck and the wreck was shrouded in "ghost nets"—fishing nets that had been lost.

We each had 16-mm film cameras and lights. In addition to the multiple challenges of cold and strong currents and risk of being entangled in netting, our biggest challenges included nitrogen narcosis and decompression sickness. On the first few dives we were diving air, wearing twin 70 cubic-foot tanks, but later we switched to a "trimix" gas of oxygen, nitrogen and helium in equal parts. We used SOS gauges (also called "Bend-O-Matics") with great caution for in-water decompression, to hopefully avoid getting bent.

I'll never forget my first dive on the *Andrea Doria*. We all made it to the deck at 170 feet just fine, but when I went to turn on my camera, nothing happened. I motioned to Al and Jack and they assumed I'd just go back up so they waved goodbye and disappeared into the wreck.

I sat there for a moment, fooling with my camera and all the sudden it worked, so I started working my way to the stern. The fishing nets might have been separated from their ships, but they were still doing their job; there were big fish, pollock, caught in the nets. Some were still alive, struggling. For some, the struggle was clearly over. I noticed fish skeletons everywhere. It was an eerie sight.

My bottom time was nearly exhausted. As I finished filming I saw Jack and Al approaching. We reach the ascent line together, with Al and Jack ascending ahead of me. As he grabs the line, Jack accidentally kicks my mask, flooding it. The cold water hits my face like a slap. Here I am, 170-feet deep on the *Andrea Doria* with a flooded mask. I have a bulky camera in one hand and a dive light in the other hand and I'm trying to clear my mask with one fist—while also keeping my arm hooked around the ascent line. To let go of the line was to risk being lost at sea. I'm burning through my air and racking up more deco time. It was terrifying.

Thankfully I managed to keep it together, clear my mask, stay in contact with the ascent line, and do my deco stops without incident. Everything worked out, but that dive was one of the scariest I've ever done.

On another dive, Al and Jack entered one of the *Andrea Doria*'s cabins and Jack emerged with a wooden plaque. On it was a plastic label that designated it as the second-class cabin. He surfaced with it and showed it to the gang on the boat and they were all excited to see it.

On the next dive, I found a similar wooden plaque; only this one had a label that read, "Premiera" on it. It was a first-class cabin label. My first thought was, "Aha. I've got one up on Al." If you know anything about Al Giddings, you know that one-upping him was not an easy thing to do. I tucked the plaque under the top of my wet suit, smiling.

Once I got back on the boat I told Al I had something special to show him. I pulled the little piece of wood out from underneath my wet suit. Unfortunately, the plastic label that read, "Premiera" had come loose and was gone. I was left holding a worm-eaten, decaying piece of wood. Everyone thought it was really funny. Except me. I still have that piece of wood, sitting on my desk.

More *Andrea Doria* antics. You have to keep in mind that on trips like this, there's a lot of down time. It's common for dives to get cancelled due to weather. And it's common for divers to get restless and start looking for some kind of trouble to get into—or pranks to play on each other.

So, Al and I had each recently gotten a pair of the latest Scubapro fins, the Revolution Jet Fin. It was one of the first vented fins, designed to allowed water to flow through them for less resistance and improved propulsion. Back then they were a source of controversy among hardcore divers. It's funny how much divers love to debate about which pair of fins—or mask, or regulator or you name it—is the very best thing, ever. Anyway, we both liked how well the fins were performing, especially in the strong currents on the Doria, so we were having a bit of fun kidding Jack about his sorry no-vent fins. He'd started to grow tired of us teasing about how our fins were better than his, so one night we took Jack's fins into the engine room, borrowed some tools and managed to punch a couple big round holes in each fin. The next morning as we all geared up for the dive, nobody said a word about Jack's fins.

Speaking of gear, when we first went aboard to meet the crew we'd be diving with, we saw a bunch of tough guys, hardcore commercial divers who'd just come straight from the oil fields. Everything about them had a hard edge, including their heavy-duty work clothes, which were stained and threadbare at the knees and elbows. They nicknamed us the "California tube suckers."

Al, Jack and I looked like city slickers compared to these cowboys, so we decided we needed to get some real work clothes, especially since in addition to the diving we were expected to help serve as boat crew and assist with topside diving operations. We went to a hardware store and bought work gloves and overalls. But everything was brand new. I don't know whose idea this was, but we were desperate to blend in, so we set about to make our new clothes look stained and worn, spilling oil on them and rubbing our gloves in the dirt.

Looking back, it was a dumb thing to do. But we were young and in over our heads a little. Somehow we managed to pull it off. I'm sure the commercial divers had us figured out by then, anyway, but nobody gave us a hard time.

Two members of the Krasberg/Zinkowski *Doria* expedition were Elgin Ciampi and Jacque Mayol. Both men were prominent in diving circles; Elgin had a reputation as a journalist and veteran wreck diver, and Mayol's claim to fame was as a world-champion deep freediver. Their "star power" helped finance the project, which included using twin Rebikoff Pegasus wet submersibles rigged with cameras. The idea was to fly the subs over the massive wreck, filming a "bird's-eye" view.

On their first attempt at using the Pegasus units, something went terribly wrong. Apparently the propulsion system on Ciampi's unit failed, and while dealing with the equipment failure he ran out of air and was forced to abort the dive. He surfaced unconscious. He was turning blue. As the support team struggled to reach Ciampi and get him on board the boat, Jacques Mayol surfaced with his Pegasus unit. He attempted to salvage Ciampi's sub by attaching it to his own, but in the confusion of Ciampi's rescue, both Pegasus units—and the cameras attached to them—drifted away and sank. They were never seen again.

Krasberg got Ciampi into the chamber, and saved his life, but the incident brought the expedition to an abrupt end.

A book about the Andrea Doria, Deep Descent: Adventure and Death on the Andrea Doria, *by Kevin F. McMurray, is available on Amazon.com.*

Camera Man

Falling In Love With Africa

By 1970 Gloria and I decided to end our marriage. Our lives had simply taken us in different directions; I'd spent a lot of time traveling for various film jobs and Gloria had built a successful career in the investment business. We parted as friends.

That same year I made my first trip to Africa, including diving off Kenya with Al Santmyer who had started Bay Travel. My son Flip traveled with me. We dived north of Mombasa and at Watamu Beach Malindi—the site of one of the very first national underwater parks established in the world. Sport diving was new at Watamu and the reserve was the first area designated as a no-take zone. Spearfishing was prohibited.

After the diving, Al Santmyer, Stan Berman, Flip and I went on a short Kenyan safari. We chartered a small plane and flew to Ngorongoro Crater in Tanzania. We landed in the middle of a field of beautiful yellow flowers. Some game rangers pulled up in an old Jeep and took us cruising around inside the crater, which is now a UNESCO World heritage Site. We saw the big five—rhinos, elephants, lions, leopard and cape buffalo—all in one short day.

After the safari, and our diving off Kenya, we met a friend from Zurich who took us to a ski area on Rathbone Mountain. Even though I'd never done it before I had the urge to ski. I wanted to see what it was like. Stan Berman, Flip and I didn't have winter clothes but we didn't let that stop us. We took a cable car and stood on the mountain in the snow in our California sport jackets and loafers. While staying at the ski resort we didn't have to work hard to fit the role of crazy American tourists—it came naturally. And it turns out I really enjoyed skiing.

By this time in my life I'd already done a lot of traveling, but there was something about this trip had a profound, lasting effect on me. It made me more aware of the world, and it made me want to do more traveling, more exploring. I've returned to Africa many times since that first trip. My wife Roz, to whom I've been married for over 24 years now, and I have led many safaris together. Africa has a special place in both our hearts.

The Egyptian Red Sea

After diving with David Doubilet in the Red Sea and meeting Howard Rosenstein at Sharm el-Sheikh, I decided to start organizing trips to Egypt's Red Sea and run them out of the Diving Locker. We were one of the first dive shops to specialize in exotic dive travel and we ended up training a lot of divers who made multiple trips to a variety of different destinations with us over the years. Having a steady clientele of repeat customers must have meant we were doing something right.

While in the Red Sea with a dive group I met Bruno Valetti, one of the great Italian documentary filmmakers. Bruno was making an underwater film off Sharm el-Sheikh and he invited our dive group to play a bit role in the film. Except this one was far from a documentary; it was a crazy action/comedy film set underwater, in a cocktail lounge. There were fake plastic creatures—sharks, big tunas and a big moray eel—on the underwater set. In the film, the moray eel attacks one of the cocktail waitresses—all of whom are serving Champagne underwater. While topless. The film was crazy, but our "15 minutes of fame" was a lot of fun. I still run into people from that trip—and they're still talking about those very impressive underwater cocktail waitresses.

Later Howard Rosenstein got in touch with me and asked if I wanted to work on a film for BBC television. Howard is a great friend and I'd done some work for Tel Aviv television in the past, so I said sure.

Howard explained that just north of Ras Mohammed, a wreck had recently been discovered in a place where very few divers ever ventured. The wreck of the *Dunraven* was discovered after it snared a fisherman's nets.

Howard had built Red Sea Divers into a successful dive business. He was well respected in the region. In fact, he'd developed a good friendship with the US Ambassador, Sam Lewis, who later was instrumental in arranging one the first peaceful exchanges between Egypt and Israel.

Anyway, Howard pitched his *Dunraven* documentary idea to the BBC, working on the premise that the *Dunraven* was rumored to be carrying gold at the time of its sinking—and that at one time Lawrence of Arabia was in Aqaba—so what if the gold had been meant to be used by Lawrence of Arabia to aid the Bedouin people? Howard knew how to whet the appetites of the talking heads of TV land. He's good at that kind of stuff.

The BBC went for it. Howard and I made a one-hour film with BBC cameraman Jack Pizzey, called *Mystery of the Red Sea Wreck*. While doing research for the film we learned that there were actually two *Dunraven* ships that sailed the area during the time of Lawrence of Arabia, and that ours wasn't even the right one.

Oh well. We did a lot of great diving on that wreck and we had a lot of fun and we made a nice little film. The Red Sea remains one of my very favorite places in the world.

"Like Diving in Tomato Soup"

Rick Rosenthal is a four-time Emmy award-winning wildlife documentary filmmaker. A marine biologist, he's one of the best in the business. And he's a close friend. I'm fortunate to have worked with him on several assignments.

One time we worked together diving in Kiska, Alaska. Rick put together a project to film a man named Charlie House, who had been assigned to serve at the U.S. Navy Weather Station on Kiska Island when the Japanese invaded in June 1942. Kiska is the next-to-last island in the Rat Islands, part of the Aleutian chain—almost to Russia. The island is 22 miles long and anywhere from 1 mile to 6 miles wide. And it's all harsh, cold, rugged wilderness.

When the Japanese invaded Kiska, they stormed the weather station, killing two men and capturing seven. Charlie was the only one who managed to escape. The Japanese launched a search for him but gave up after several days, figuring he'd have died of exposure by then. Charlie survived in the wild, in bitter cold conditions, for nearly two months before surrendering. He'd nearly starved to death. After surrendering he was sent to a Japanese prisoner of war camp.

Besides Rick and myself, the third person on our crew was still photographer Charlie Arneson. Charlie was a graduate student at Scripps at the time. Some of his research had him working with the Navy studying how bioluminescence affects the detection of submarines. Incidentally, Charlie decided he'd had enough of academia and decided that when he finished grad school he wanted to be in the film business. He's really in it now; he works as Hollywood's Jim Cameron's right-hand man.

Anyway, Charlie House's saga was only a part of the story. The main theme of the film centered on just how close the Japanese had come to reaching the Alaskan mainland during World War II, and how important it was for the U.S. Navy, with help from allied Canadian forces, to defeat the Japanese and regain control of Kiska and Attu Islands. During the battle, our Navy sunk a lot of Japanese cargo and military ships and a couple submarines. The Japanese finally accepted defeat on July 28, 1943.

I don't know how true this is, but I think it's a safe bet that we were about the only ones who'd ever explored those wrecks. If we weren't the only ones, we were among the few, that's for sure. One of the more exciting dives I made with Charlie Arneson was on a small Japanese submarine sunk at about 130 feet. The water temperature was actually below freezing—about 28 or 29 degrees—so we were using dry suits. I had a bad cold at the time, but we had a chance to make this submarine dive and it was an important part of the film. We just had to do it.

Before entering the water, I let Charlie know I might have a hard time clearing my ears. We made the dive just fine, though. I didn't have any trouble clearing. We did have to go through a plankton bloom on the way down, though. It turned the water solid red, with no visibility whatsoever. It was like diving in tomato soup. Really cold tomato soup.

We anchored on the wreck and because there was a strong current running we made sure to descend and ascend on the anchor line. The Aleutians are not where you'd want to go drifting off. Our large motor sailor was the only boat around.

We made the dive without incident, but on the way up I got about 20 feet from the surface and I felt a sharp pain, like a knife being jabbed in my ear and sinuses. Because of my cold I had a reverse block. The pain was intense and the block was causing me loss of equilibrium. I felt like I was spinning. I signaled to Charlie to stick with me. I didn't know how long I was going to be hanging there; I thought I might need him to share air, or go get more tanks. Charlie stayed with me, hanging on the line, until I was finally able to clear the reverse block.

Camera Man

I was glad to reach the surface after that experience.

Of course, we had a few other challenges, too. The water conditions in the Bering Sea are often dangerous. We ran into extreme weather— high winds and huge waves—while we were underway to Attu Island. And as it turns out, the skipper of the motor sailor was an alcoholic (and he was probably mental, too). Charlie and Rick took over running the boat. At one point the waves were so high that we feared they might capsize the boat, so we got into our dry suits, just in case the boat went down.

That was an exciting adventure.

In Search of the Coelacanth

According to an article on *National Geographic*'s web site, "The primitive-looking coelacanth was thought to have gone extinct with the dinosaurs 65 million years ago. But its discovery in 1938 by a South African museum curator on a local fishing trawler fascinated the world and ignited a debate about how this bizarre lobe-finned fish fits into the evolution of land animals.

There are only two known species of coelacanths: one that lives near the Comoros Islands off the east coast of Africa, and one found in the waters off Sulawesi, Indonesia. Many scientists believe that the unique characteristics of the coelacanth represent an early step in the evolution of fish to terrestrial four-legged animals like amphibians."

In the early 1970s San Francisco's Steinhart Aquarium and *National Geographic* teamed up to support an expedition to the Comoros Islands off Mozambique, in search of the mysterious coelacanth. I got hired as one of the cameramen, once again working with Al Giddings.

I knew we'd be doing a lot of deep diving, below 250 feet. One Sunday before we started on the project I decided I wanted to see what the diving was like during the day before we started making these deep night dives, so I asked one of our young helpers to make a dive with me. The conditions were perfect; the water was warm, clear and calm. When we got to about 125 feet, I motioned for my young dive buddy to stay put while I went deeper. I zipped straight down the wall to 275 feet. I had my still camera with me, a Nikon F in Al Giddings' Niko-mar housing. When I leveled off I looked around and noticed a strange-looking angelfish. Knowing that I shouldn't waste a lot of time at that deep depth I fired off a few shots, wondering if the effects of nitrogen narcosis would show up in the photos. After that I started making my way back up the wall. The kid waiting at 125 feet was glad to see me. And the photos? Turns out they were sharp and in focus.

Our team included scientist John McCosker and aquarist Dave Powell from Steinhart. John was optimistic that we'd be able to bring back a live coelacanth, but that didn't work out. He did settle for obtaining a specimen preserved in formaldehyde.

It was on the coelacanth expedition that we made the discovery of photoblepharon, which are small fish that have a fluorescent patch in the eye. In the dark it blinks like a firefly.

We first discovered these when Al and I were deep diving at night looking for Coelacanths. We made dives to 220 feet and a bit deeper along the wall using underwater scooters. We were cruising along the wall one night and when I noticed the strange lights I poked Al and motioned for him to shut off his dive light. Later he told me he thought I'd lost my mind, but he shut the light off anyway. It looked like we were in outer space. The water was pitch black and there were thousands of photoblepharon surrounding us, flashing. It was surreal.

Later the crew from Steinhart and Dr. Sylvia Earle discovered photoblepharon at shallower depths and were able to collect some for display at Steinhart. These were the first ever to be shown in aquaria.

After one of our deep coelacanth-hunting dives Al and I typically spent quite a lot of time decompressing. We'd park the scooters in about 15 to 20 feet of water and just lay there on the bottom for an hour or more. We both had Scubapro SOS meters, although we were sort of on our own in terms of a reliable deco schedule. We turned off our dive lights to conserve the batteries. The boat was nearby, waiting for us, so every once in a while we'd turn on our dive lights to let them know we were still okay. Our system was crude at best, but it worked.

As I said earlier, the most exciting diving I've ever done was on the *Andrea Doria*, but this diving with the coelacanths in the depths of the Comoros runs a close second.

It wasn't just the diving that proved challenging. During our expedition, a cholera epidemic swept the island. One of our assistants was a local fisherman, a big strapping man, and all muscle. He looked as fit as could be, but he came down with cholera and died within three days. Our team decided we should leave at once. But not, of course, until we'd celebrated our accomplishments with a wrap party. The champagne flowed and John McCosker was the first to jump from the hotel's second story balcony into the pool.

Incidentally, a few years back, French marine biologist and underwater photographer Laurent Ballesta partnered with *National Geographic* and Blancpain on a coelacanth expedition to Sodwana, South Africa. Using sophisticated mixed-gas systems Ballesta and his team routinely reached 350 to 400 feet, and in some instances ventured as deep as 610 feet. They succeeded in capturing stunning coelacanth imagery, and Ballesta's team conducted research critical to understanding more about this mysterious fish.

The dive team staged waterproof iPads along their deco lines to they could play games and watch movies during lengthy decompression stops. That's a far cry from how we did it in the '70s—back before Ballesta and his team members were even born.

Tales from *The Deep*

By the mid- to late-1970s things were going pretty well. The Diving Locker was chugging along and I'd been staying busy working as a cameraman. My next big step in the world of Hollywood filmmaking came about, once again, due to Al Giddings. Filming was starting on Peter Benchley's next novel, *The Deep*. Benchley, who wrote *Jaws*, was a good friend of Stan Waterman's. Stan and Al were co-directors for the underwater filming and I hired on as a camerman. We made a good team.

The story was set in Bermuda, but we started filming underwater scenes in the British Virgin Islands before moving to Bermuda, and Australia before returning to finish the film in Bermuda.

Our underwater scenes in the British Virgin Islands were filmed on the wreck of the RMS *Rhone*, which broke into two parts and sunk off Salt Island during a hurricane in 1867. The bow section rests in 80 feet of water while the stern is in about 30 feet.

The film starred Jacqueline Bisset, Nick Nolte and Robert Shaw. All were deeply committed to their work as actors. Jackie, in addition to being beautiful and sexy, is a quiet, elegant person. Robert Shaw was a great actor with a larger-than-life personality. Nick Nolte might have a bit of a crazy streak but he was great to work with. And Peter Benchley had a bit role, too, appearing as a mate aboard the boat. While in the British Virgin Islands we based out of the Peter Island Beach Resort and Spa, which is a very posh resort. We traveled by fast boat to the *Rhone* dive site each day, where our support boat, the *Moby*, was waiting for us. The small boat skipper was very safety conscious and didn't like the way we walked around while the boat was underway. He was constantly after us to stay seated. Our friend Jack McKenney, who was working as a stunt double for Nick Nolte, was tired of being reprimanded. One morning Jack suggested we all "fall" overboard just to drive the skipper crazy. Just like that, we all jumped overboard. I thought the poor skipper would have a heart attack.

Even though all the actors were trained to dive—and were pretty good at it, too—stunt doubles are routinely used for portions of the filming. One scene called for Jackie's character to probe an area of the wreck, reaching under it with a stick, when a big moray eel grabs the stick. We shot the scene several times using the stunt double and we came away with some good footage, but when we looked at the dailies, Jackie didn't like the scene because the double's arms didn't appear as toned and muscular as hers. She said, "Wait a minute, that doesn't even look like me. Her arms look too flabby." The next day, Jackie did all the diving scenes herself. And she did a great job.

All our close-up and wreck interior shots were filmed in Bermuda on a set that was built and then sunk inside a huge, 35-foot deep saltwater tank. One scene required filming with sharks, so we hired fishermen to catch a few good-sized sharks that we could put in the tank. Unfortunately, the sharks didn't fare so well after being caught and transported to our set. They were nearly dead by the time we started filming, so we had our camera assistants pick them up and sort of push the sharks in front of the camera so we could get a few close shots. It didn't work very well, but we made the best of it.

As we were breaking for lunch everyone was climbing out of the tank and the sharks were just lying on the bottom. I asked, "Hey, what do we do with the sharks?" but everyone on the set just sort of looked at me and shrugged. The tank had a pump that circulated seawater through it, so I dragged the sharks over and put them in front of the pipe that supplied the water, and then I joined the others for lunch.

When we returned to the set there was a lot of noise and confusion— the sharks had come back to life! It seems that all they needed was a bit of seawater rushing over their gills. The carpenters and artists

Camera Man

working on building the framework for an underwater set were standing on the framework and were all excited because of the sharks. They feared that if somebody fell in the tank they'd be attacked and eaten. I thought the whole thing was hilarious.

When working on a movie set, there's always a lot of down time spent just waiting around for something to happen. It wasn't uncommon for us to reach the set at the crack of dawn and not actually get down to work until after 10 a.m.

Al is always very organized and he makes sure his film sets are that way, too. He made sure our crew sheds had several large workbenches where we could set up our cameras. They were each about six feet long and plenty wide, with a wooden shelf underneath—the perfect place for a nice long nap. I made a deal with fellow crewmembers Bob Cecchini and Jack Monestier to wake me as soon as it was time to get started.

My father always said, "Don't stand up if you can sit down. Don't sit down if you can lie down. And don't stay awake if you can sleep." That might sound lazy, but in fact it's sound advice. After a nap I'd be all fresh and ready to work and others had been walking around, sitting in the sun, checking their watches and getting frustrated. It was just better to jump out from underneath the camera bench, all rested and enthusiastic and not upset about the wait. In the film business you have to be a good guy and not be a complainer if you expect to have a good relationship with the crew and management.

We spent some long days at that tank. A bus would take us back to the hotel in the evening. Nick Nolte refused to ride in the bus and had a motor scooter. I remember producer Peter Gruber being worried that Nick might get hurt and screw up the timing of the filming.

One night after dark we were on our way to the hotel and Nick was behind the bus on his scooter, with his girlfriend who had just arrived. Jack McKenney went to the back of the bus and gave Nick a "pressed ham"—he pulled his pants down and pressed his butt against the rear window. At the next stop, everyone is watching and here comes Nick and his girlfriend on the scooter. As they passed us Nick's girlfriend pulls up the back of her dress and we all could see her bare rear end as they drove off. It was a fitting end to another crazy day in the film industry.

Nick Nolte was a character, but he was great to work with. He even did some of the more strenuous underwater scenes himself. I was impressed with his diving skills.

When we were preparing to leave for Australia for more filming on *The Deep*, Al called me and said he wanted to hire someone to spear fish to help attract the sharks. I immediately thought of Howard Hall, who was working for me at the Diving Locker at that time and often dived with me when we were filming blue and mako sharks. I told Al he'd be perfect for the job, so Howard came to Australia to spear fish for the grey reef shark scenes. Grey reefs are probably responsible for more shark attacks than any other shark. Not shark deaths, but shark bites.

Howard and Stan Waterman immediately hit if off. In fact, Stan later hired Howard to work with him on some other projects. And Howard went on to become a highly successful underwater cameraman and film producer. He has received many Emmys and other awards for his underwater film work. I'm very proud of his accomplishments.

The Fairmount Southampton Resort was our base in Bermuda. Some of the crew rented apartments or little cottages but most of the principals stayed at the hotel and we'd usually meet in the lobby and go to dinner together. One night we all met as usual, but I told them to go ahead without me. That night I had a dinner date with Jackie Bisset. We took a shuttle to a nice place across the golf course from the Southampton, where we met Jack McKenney and a lady friend of his. We had a nice evening together, and as the evening was winding down Jack suggested we walk back to the Southampton, which sounded like a nice idea, but it had rained earlier in the day and the grass was wet, and toads—lots of toads—were hopping all over the place. It wasn't a particularly romantic end to the evening.

I became fond of Jackie during the filming. I thought she was special. The crew helped celebrate her birthday at a party where everyone was asked to wear white. That night Jackie asked me to dance with her and we circled the dance floor like it was a movie scene. I decided I liked this Hollywood film production business.

One afternoon Jackie and I rented scooters for a trip to Hamilton Town to go shopping. The little scooters had small baskets on the handlebars. While Jackie was in a store, I bought a red rose and stuck it in her basket. Her French boyfriend arrived in Bermuda the next day. My special friendship with Jackie was just that—a friendship.

Over the years people have asked me about filming *The Deep*. I typically get asked about the scenes in which Jackie is shown diving wearing a white t-shirt. An obviously wet, white t-shirt. They ask, did you see her? And I tell them yes, I saw her. I filmed her. Jackie looked fantastic in that t-shirt, but she did not enjoy being exploited because of her sexuality. But the image of Jackie in the wet t-shirt became iconic to the film.

When it was all done we'd worked on the film for 153 days. We spent 8,010 hours underwater, with underwater footage comprising 40 percent of the film. On the last day that Robert Shaw was going to be available, we had to do a close-up shot where he appeared to be entangled in the spear gun line and in danger of being bitten by a giant moray eel. We had a real moray eel that was one of the biggest eels that I have ever seen. Believe it or not, it was a "rental eel" obtained from the Shedd Aquarium in Chicago. We used it in the close ups. We had a fake eel for the long shots.

Robert Shaw arrived on the set in the morning and had his own little chalet, actually a plywood shack and sat there most of the day, visiting with one of his friends from Bermuda. Apparently the two men consumed a considerable amount of rum while waiting for Robert's call to be filmed. When it came time to get Robert's close-up shots, he was drunk. But he was determined to perform. I was sitting on the edge of the tank waiting for the powers that be to make a decision, when Robert came over, saying, "Chuck, I really need that close up done right. This is what it's all about in the film business, the close-up shot. The audience needs to see my face, my eyes, in that dive mask. They need to know that it's Robert Shaw." Even though he was clearly drunk, they decided to let him do the scene. Al took him into the water by hand and set him up in front of the eel cave. One of the other divers carried Al's camera so he could concentrate on getting Robert safely into position. I'd gone in ahead of time to get my camera set up. We shot a couple angles of close ups of his face, signaled "ok" and then held onto him as we returned him to the surface. Once he sobered up a bit he left for the airport to catch a flight back to the states.

That's the way it happened in the film; Robert Shaw's wild-eyed look wasn't because of the giant eel. It was the rum.

Besides our having a few quick chats from time to time, I never really had much chance to know Robert Shaw, but I thought he was truly a fine actor, one of the great characters of film history.

Trouble and Treasure
in Truk Lagoon

Starting in the early 1970s I made several trips to Micronesia to dive Truk Lagoon, now known as Chuuk. The area consists of eleven major islands and dozens of smaller ones, strung together by a fringing coral reef.

During World War II, Japan used these islands as the main base for their naval operations and was one of their most formidable strongholds in the Pacific until February 1944, when a U.S. air strike code-named "Operation Hailstone" rained down on the Japanese fleet, sinking at least 12 Japanese warships and 32 merchant ships.

Jacques Cousteau and his team first explored the area in 1969. His 1971 television documentary about the "Ghost Fleet of Truk Lagoon" quickly made the lagoon a "must see" destination for wreck diver. In 1973, Chuuk native Kimiuo Aisek, who was 17 when he witnessed "Operation Hailstone," opened the first dive shop, Blue Lagoon Dive Shop. He was one of the first to explore the wrecks, and we became good friends over the years. He remained a driving force in preserving the wrecks and promoting tourism to Chuuk until his death in 2001 at age 73. In 2014, the Kimiuo Aisek Memorial Museum opened. It houses Micronesia's greatest collection of nautical artifacts and local art.

Many of the wrecks were found by pilots from Air Micronesia, who noted the position of oil slicks in the lagoon as they approached the landing strip. I was visiting Kimiuo when pilots Keith Jaeger and Ed O'Quinn came into the dive shop to ask about exploring a possible wreck site. Flight attendant Frankie Hebert and I joined them. We were probably the first divers ever to visit the deep wreck of the *Fujisan Maru*.

Kimiuo and I made several more dives together on the *Fujisan*. On one dive I found a small porcelain vase, decorated with a delicate pattern of blue flowers. Here it was among all this wreckage, such a fragile item, in perfect condition. I picked it up and showed it to Kimiuo, then carefully returned it to the wreck.

Later, as we were hanging on the line doing our decompression stop, Kimiuo tapped me on the arm, removed the vase from his BC pocket and handed it to me, as a gesture of our friendship. It was a special moment.

While on assignment photographing Chuuk's shipwrecks with Dr. Sylvia Earle and Al Giddings for *National Geographic*, we explored several other deep wrecks. During that trip Al started feeling pain and numbness, which are the symptoms of decompression sickness. He knocked on my hotel room door late one night and suggested we take a trip to the local hospital.

The hospital was definitely Third World, but it did have a recompression chamber. Even though Al wasn't feeling well, he went over the chamber, checking the fittings, supply hoses and seals, and said it looked like it would work. Sylvia went over the *US Navy Diving Manual* and decided our best option was to treat Al on a Table Four air-only decompression schedule, so we got Kimiuo to supply us with enough compressed air, stuffed Al into the coffin-sized recompression chamber and hoped for the best. Nearly 12 hours later, Al emerged. He was tired, but he wasn't bent.

One particular dive with Al on the "Ghost Fleet of Truk Lagoon" is one I will never forget. We were on the *Aikoku Maru*, which is about 200 feet deep. We entered the ship's hull at 180 feet and turned towards the stern. The ship was leaning at an angle, with wires hanging down and debris everywhere. We passed though one compartment after another, inching our way through the tight passageways. Al had the camera and I was handling the movie lights, which were attached to a long cable lowered down from the boat. As I scanned the passageway, I noticed bumps sticking up from what looked like a thick layer of ashes on the floor. It took me a moment to realize that the bumps

Camera Man

were human skulls—the remains of Japanese soldiers. I looked closer. Bones were strewn everywhere. It was a chilling site.

As we turned to make our way out of the ship, we realized our visibility had gone to zero. There was so much silt that my movie lights were of little use to illuminate our path—but proved to be an important lifeline—as the only way we were able to make it out of the wreck was to feel our way out by following the light cable. Al put his hand on my shoulder as we made our way to the opening in the hull.

I was glad to finally see the light from the opening in the wreck, and to see our safety divers waiting outside with additional tanks. We had a pretty lengthy decompression stop after that one, but I didn't mind.

Note: The remains of Japanese soldiers lost in the battle at Chuuk Lagoon have since been recovered and have been cremated.

When Real Life Is Better Than in the Movies

The life I was living was pretty great; I had exciting work as an underwater cameraman that had me mingling with the Hollywood crowd and offered me the chance to travel and dive all over the world. I had recently been named as the Bachelor of the Month in a 1973 issue of *Cosmopolitan* magazine and was enjoying bachelor life. I remember we had just wrapped up filming on *The Deep* and I returned home feeling like I'd finally realized my dream of making it in the film business. I was fit and tan, my hair was long, and I was driving a brand new blue Porsche. My life was everything I'd dreamed it could be.

And then I pulled into the parking lot of a Von's supermarket and I noticed a beautiful girl in a car just ahead of me. We each parked and went into the store. She had long brown hair and dark brown eyes, and was very slim. She was beautiful. But more than that, she had a way about her that I found captivating. Being a bit bashful I didn't start a conversation with her right away, We passed each other in the grocery store aisles a few times, when finally she said hello. I broke out in a big smile right there in the frozen food section.

She said her name was Roz. I'm not even sure I told her my name. I just remember holding up this frozen carrot cake with a logo of a little house on the carton. I asked her if she'd ever tried this brand and she said no, but she took one from the freezer and said she'd try it. Okay, so it was an awkward conversation, but it was a start. As we got to the checkout line I believe I made one of the best decisions of my life—I asked her if she would have dinner with me sometime. She said sure and we exchanged numbers.

I think the next weekend we went to the Chart House for our first date. It took us 22 years after that first date before we finally married. Now that we've been married for more than 24 years we both look back and wonder why it took us so long. But the thing is, we each had a lot going on in our lives when we first met. We'd see each other for a while and then I'd go off on a film job, and she'd go on with her life and work. We continued dating off and on all those years. At one point Roz met a man she intended to marry, but that didn't work out. She became a single mom and was busy raising her daughter, Heather. But we'd still run into each other from time to time and we'd pick up right where we left off. We traveled together a lot and always had a great time. Again, this went on for 22 years.

Finally, I had just come back from working on *The Abyss* when we were out one evening and she delivered an ultimatum. I thought she was kidding at first, but she wasn't. Roz told me that she loved me very much but that she wasn't content to be my "main squeeze" and that remaining in our relationship was probably preventing her from meeting someone who wanted more. We broke up for the final time.

A few days later, I left to work on a training film for Scuba Schools International (SSI). With me on that assignment was a close friend of mine, Charlie Arneson. We'd worked together for many years, and Charlie knew Roz, and liked her. Charlie and I were sitting on the beach one evening after the shoot and I shared with him that Roz had given me an ultimatum. I told him it shook me up, and that I actually was pretty serious and was thinking of settling down with Roz. That's when Charlie looked at me like I was crazy and said, "Chuck, what are you doing? Roz is great and everything, but you are traveling around the world you have everything going for you—a fun exciting life, you're doing just what you want, there are girls in every port—why would you want to settle down?" I sort of shrugged it off, and quickly changed the subject.

Later, when I returned home to La Jolla I was still confused. There is a sea wall near my home at the beach where I would go to sit and watch the sunsets. I went there and all I could see was couples. A lot of couples. They were walking around holding hands, kissing. I remember feeling very alone. It had been about three months since I had seen Roz, so I decided to call her and asked how she was doing. She thanked me for calling but told me she was dating someone and wanted to see how things went. I talked her into joining me for dinner at the Manhattan, an Italian steakhouse. She refused at first, but I told her I had something important to tell her. She showed up wearing a red silk blouse and a black leather mini skirt. She looked beautiful. We made some small talk and then after a few glasses of wine, I just blurted it out, "Roz, I've been thinking about it, and I think we should get married." She almost fell out of her chair, and I was holding onto mine with both hands.

And she said … she'd need time to think about it. Thankfully, a few weeks later she gave me a conditional yes; she'd agree to marry me if I made a proper marriage proposal—which I knew meant a diamond solitaire and me down on one knee. I took her to dinner at George's Restaurant, a very classy fine-dining restaurant on the water in La Jolla. I ended up on one knee in the middle of George's and I must have made a proper proposal, because she said yes! The restaurant owner, George, was there and he very thoughtfully ordered Champagne, and everyone there was congratulating us and wishing us well.

It wasn't long before Roz and her daughter Heather moved into my home in La Jolla. Heather was only 8 or 9 years old at the time. I was a little nervous about having a young child in my life, but Heather proved to be a great addition, because it wasn't just Roz and me as a couple. We became a family.

Roz and I each are very independent people, so we talked about how we'd need to trust each other and accept each other's individuality and independence. Roz knew I'd still be traveling a lot for my film work and she intended to continue working for Pacific Bell, where she was a legal assistant.

It took us a couple of years of being engaged before we figured everything out. And then finally, we got married. Our friend, Sammy

Ledeki is a very successful restaurateur. He hosted our wedding at his beautiful new home high up on a hillside in La Jolla. He took care of the whole thing, including all the catering for the reception. Everything was perfect.

Well after all these years, it has worked out for us. I love Roz with every bone in my body. She is good for me. We have traveled all over the world together, diving and having the greatest adventures. We work well together planning group trips; I handle logistics and Roz takes care of the PR and advertising. We're a good team. Our marriage is my life's greatest adventure.

These days I am walking a little slower than I used to, and Roz has been good about adjusting her pace, and our schedule. But we're still traveling all the time, and we still have a lot of future plans for diving, land trips, cruises, etc. We both are into photography, she shoots stills and I am still shooting video. I could go on and on talking about Roz. She is the most important part of my life.

On Going Silent

'd really enjoyed filming southern right whales off Patagonia with Bill Curtsinger, so when Al Giddings expressed interest in filming humpback whales in Hawaii, I made sure he knew I'd jump at the chance to join him.

Al contacted Anglia Productions in the United Kingdom and sold them on filming a one-hour special on humpback whales. I'd worked with Dr. Roger Payne on the right whale project and we'd both worked with Dr. Sylvia Earle on the coelacanth project. The two researchers joined us in the filming of *Gentle Giants of the Pacific*.

We spent more than a month filming in Hawaii, where humpback whales congregate in late fall and winter to mate and raise young after spending the summer months in Alaskan waters feeding on krill. The west side of Maui is a reliable place to find humpbacks, as neighboring islands Molokai, Lanai and Kahoolawe provide a buffer from Pacific storms.

We worked from a Zodiac inflatable and also from Tad Lucky's 40-foot sport fishing boat, spending long hours waiting and searching for the whales. The pace of documentary filming is very different than doing a Hollywood thriller, but there's still a lot of waiting involved. Patience is paramount in the film business. Sometimes when we got into the water we could hear them singing, even though we couldn't see them.

One new development in our documentary filming on this trip was the use of rebreathers. We had a pair of Emerson closed-circuit oxygen rebreathers. They were perfect for getting close to the whales, because with this type of rebreather there are no exhaust bubbles like there are on a regular open-circuit scuba rig. Without exhaust bubbles the unit is practically silent and since the whales were skittish around boats and around us, too, we felt like using the rebreathers might give us a bit of an advantage when filming.

There was one potential problem with the rebreathers, though. And it was a big one; pure oxygen becomes toxic below 30 feet, causing seizures and unconsciousness—usually without warning. If either happens underwater, a diver will likely die.

We conditioned ourselves to pay close attention to our depth, which I have to admit wasn't easy, given that we were out in blue water with no bottom for reference, and the fact that filming the whales was such an incredible experience—it was easy to become distracted and not pay careful attention to my depth gauge.

On one occasion I was getting some great shots of Al filming a female humpback and her young calf, that's exactly what happened. I went underneath them to get the shot from a different angle. It was great stuff. Then I noticed Al above me, frantically waving his arms, signaling me to come up, come up. I hadn't paid careful attention to my depth, and sure enough, when I looked at my gauge it read 60 feet. I was in danger of oxygen poisoning. I quickly ascended to a safe depth—and stayed above 30 feet for the rest of the dive. I was lucky that time. I'm glad I didn't go silent.

Roaming on *Nomads of the Deep*

In 1978 I joined the team of an IMAX film called *Nomads of the Deep*, which was to include footage of humpback whales, and several shark species including blues and makos. IMAX is an acronym for Image MAXimum, which is a motion picture file format that has the capacity to record and display images of far greater resolution than conventional film systems. Films shot in super-large IMAX format must be shown in special theatres. The film was produced by the IMAX Company, with Canadian John Stoneman as writer/producer and director. My son Flip, an accomplished underwater still photographer, was also on our crew. Incidentally, this film assignment ultimately led him to work as a photographer for *National Geographic*—a position that turned into a 30-year career. David Douglas, from IMAX, served both as the camera tech and topside cameraman.

Our itinerary included filming locations in Hawaii, the Red Sea, and San Diego. Our first stop was the island of Maui, where we chartered Tad Lucky's boat, out of Lahaina. The first challenge we faced was how to get the massive IMAX camera in and out of the water. It weighed over 350 pounds, and Tad's boat, while open across the stern, had no hoist or crane. We improvised, using a thick sheet of plywood as a sort of sled. We tied ropes to the plywood and fastened the camera to it using door latches. Two guys would stay on deck holding the ropes while Flip and I would slide the camera into the water. Once we got the camera in the water we'd undo the latches, take the camera and swim away with it. When our filming was finished the guys would slide the plywood back into the water, we'd fasten the camera down and they'd haul it back onboard. It was a crude system, especially for such a sophisticated (and expensive) camera, but it worked.

Once we got the camera in the water is was slightly buoyant, so that if a problem occurred while filming, the camera would slowly rise to the surface. The thing was gigantic. Flip insisted that I got the job simply because I was the only one with arms long enough to reach around the camera. Its size made the IMAX camera tricky to use, plus it lacked a monitor. I did all my filming through a basic viewfinder.

But I'm not complaining, because my job as the cameraman was nothing compared to that of David Douglas, whose job it was to load the massive 1,000-foot film magazines into the camera. Each film load lasted long enough for only three minutes of footage. Believe me when I say we had to make every second count.

Things on the IMAX shoot got slightly more complicated when we left Hawaii and moved to Sharm el-Sheikh, on Israel's Sinai Peninsula to film a reef called The Temple, which was considered to be a prime example of the Red Sea's incredible biodiversity. Our project had a lot of moving parts, including dozens and dozens of cases of film. The cases were insulated to (hopefully) protect the unexposed film from the Sinai's extreme heat.

We needed to see the results of our filming, which meant shipping the exposed film to the United States for developing, and then we'd have the dailies shipped back to Israel so we could see the results. None of this would have been possible without the help of Howard Rosenstein from Red Sea Divers. He waded through a lot of bureaucratic red tape on our behalf.

To view the processed film meant driving 130 miles to a theatre in Eliat. Driving back and forth at night and then diving all day made for an exhausting schedule.

Next, we returned to San Diego to film blue sharks, which was a piece of cake compared to being on location in Israel. The blue shark footage was easy to get. Blue sharks are beautiful creatures, but as sharks go, they don't appear to be menacing.

I haven't seen *Nomads of the Deep* in decades, but I do remember being very pleased with the film. It was on that film that we got some of the first really good large-format footage of humpback whales. I am happy to have been a part of that film.

"No Problem" in Papua New Guinea

I went to Papau New Guinea for the first time in 1988, with my friend Charlie Arneson. Charlie was a grad student at Scripps at the time, and was diving in New Guinea collecting sponges for cancer research at a research station in Madang, which is in northern Papua New Guinea. I brought a group of divers from the Diving Locker. Now, Papua New Guinea is known for some incredible diving, but this particular area didn't represent the region's best diving. It was getting a little boring after a few days, then one evening a live-aboard dive boat, the *Ocean Explorer*, which was owned by Ron and Valerie Taylor and skippered by a character named Alan Rabbe. They'd been out diving some remote islands off the coast with a group of divers led by Chris Newbert, who is an outstanding underwater photographer. His book, *Within a Rainbowed Sea* is an award-winning bestseller. Chris and his group were raving about the incredible diving they'd just done.

After Chris' group left, we sat in the bar with Alan Rabbe, drinking rum with both hands. Not me, but Alan.

Anyway, I wanted to get my divers out to those great dive sites, so I asked Alan if I could charter the boat for a few days. Alan didn't really want to do it, as he was looking forward to a few days off before taking the boat back to Australia, but he finally agreed. He said, "Okay, Chuck. I'll do it. I'll do it for you. Have your group here by 10 o'clock tonight." I asked if he thought he'd be sober enough to run the boat but he just waved his hand in the air and said, " No problem. Don't worry about it. I'll be fine."

When we boarded the *Ocean Explorer* that night, Alan didn't appear to have sobered up one bit. In fact, he seemed just as drunk as he'd been several hours before. A few people in our group rolled their eyes, whispering under their breath, "What has Chuck gotten us into now," but Alan insisted everything would be okay. "I'm fine. I'll get us out of the harbor and you can take over the boat so I can get some sleep. Now, let's get going." So, that's what we did. One of the guys in our group was a Navy man who thought it'd be great fun to skipper the boat while Alan slept off his rum.

We woke Alan before we reached the islands and he had us in the water shortly after sunrise. His pre-dive briefing went sort of like, "You all know how to dive, so stick together, don't do anything stupid, and be back on the boat in an hour." He continued, "Go down the anchor line, swim until you see a big yellow sponge and then turn left. You'll see schools of barracudas and manta rays. It'll be a wonderful dive. Wake me up when you get back."

He was right. It was wonderful. My group was happy that I'd made the decision to charter the boat.

That was the start of my diving—and my friendship—with Alan off Papua New Guinea. It's a beautiful place, with some of the best reefs in the world. I've returned there at least a dozen times to dive with Alan off his boat, the MV *FeBrina*.

Filming in Circles—
Disney's Circle Vision 360°

The Imagineers at Walt Disney came up with a film technique called Circle-Vision 360° that consisted of seven cameras oriented in a circle, shooting into mirrors to create a 360-degree image. The system was about six feet high and six feet wide and weighed at least a ton. In 1978 Al Giddings contracted me to work with him on an underwater Circle-Vision 360° film to be released at Tokyo Disneyland.

The scope of this film project was even bigger than the camera system. It was a global deal that had us traveling to South Australia to film great white sharks, Tahiti to film the black pearl farms and the hundreds of grey reef sharks found in Tahitian waters, to Micronesia's Truk Lagoon for World War II shipwrecks and coral reefs, back to the states to San Clemente Island to film the kelp forests, and to the Bahamas to film a submarine.

In Tahiti we were based on a freighter that ran supplies to the outer islands of the Tuamotos. The boat had a crane, which we used to launch and recover the huge Circle-Vision 360°camera. On a shark dive in the Apataki channel we allowed one of the tech assistants to dive with us. He was crazy about the camera and was also excited to do a shark dive. This particular dive is noted for consistently strong currents and hundreds of sharks. It lived up to its reputation—the current was ripping and there were sharks everywhere. When we got back on board the freighter after the dive, I asked the tech what he thought about the sharks. As it turns out, he was so intent on watching us filming with the Circle-Vision camera that he claimed he didn't even notice the sharks!

When the freighter unloaded the supplies it took on a cargo of copra, which is coconut meat. Well, within no time the copra starts getting real ripe and attracts large numbers of black flies. They were everywhere. It was so bad that we would put big fans at each end of the dinner table to control the flies. Each time the fan would swing away the flies would descend on our dinners. We struggled to get a bite of food without getting a mouthful of flies. It's not always glamorous in the film business.

In the Bahamas our subject was the Harbor Branch Oceanographic Institute's submersible. Filming with the Circle Vision was tricky because if you were below the camera you appeared in the frame, so we had to work from above our film subjects. Al would turn the camera on and the swim up above it, out of the frame. The rest of our team would position themselves above Al. It felt strange to be filming that way.

One day the submersible pilot, Don Liberatore, was planning to make a deep test dive and he said there was room for one observer. Everyone in the film crew wanted to make the deep dive, so we drew straws. I was the lucky one who got to make the sub dive with Don. Incidentally, Don and his wife Shirley Pomponi became close friends. We've traveled many places in the world together.

Disney's Circle Vision camera crew was responsible for assembling the 35-mm cameras and installing them in the huge housing, but Al Giddings was intent on making sure everything went as planned so he took on some of the responsibility for seeing that the housing was properly prepared before it went into the water. As you can imagine, there are lots of o-rings and lots of bolts to turn.

When on location at south Australia's Dangerous Reef, we were fortunate enough to attract several large great white sharks, which were the subject of this shoot. One shark in particular was just massive—and wasn't the slightest bit shy of coming in for a close look at the shark cage. Al's goal was to get underwater Circle Vision footage of a great white attacking a dummy on a surfboard while a topside cameraman shot the scene from the boat. We definitely had at least one shark that appeared willing to cooperate, so Al and the Disney guys finished loading the Circle Vision cameras into the housing. Al tightened the final bolts and gave the housing a pat as the crew loaded it onto a hoist. We were good to go. I entered the shark cage as the camera was being hoisted into the water, when all the sudden the shark started banging up against the cage. I started yelling, "Stop! Stop!" At first everyone thought I was yelling because of the shark, but it wasn't that at all. I was yelling because I noticed seawater pouring into the camera housing. It was leaking, and all the 35-mm Arriflex cameras were being ruined.

There was no one in the world that felt worse about it than Al, but he wasn't about to give up. He and everyone on the technical team spent the next few days drying, cleaning and repairing the cameras and somehow they got the whole thing up and running again. That's the thing about Al. He never quits.

Behind the Scenes of
For Your Eyes Only

My next big Hollywood production gig came in 1981, when Al Giddings and I worked together on the James Bond film, *For Your Eyes Only*. We were on location on New Providence in the Bahamas for four months, working with Cubby Broccoli, who was the director and producer of the James Bond films at that time. He and the crew were from England, and they were a great bunch of folks to work with. While there, our production base was the tug boat *Moby*, a boat that by now was like a second home, as Al and I had worked from the *Moby's* deck while filming *The Deep* and several other big projects. The *Moby* was anchored off Lyford Cay on the backside of New Providence. Our shore-based home was the Coral Harbour Beach Villas, which were condos right on the beach. They had small kitchens and patios, which was better than staying in a hotel room for months at a time. The crew and cast got along well, and we'd often get together for dinner or drinks at Coral Harbour after a day of filming.

Roger Moore played James Bond in *For Your Eyes Only*. Even though we were on the set for months, I never actually met him.

It was common for VIPs to visit the set during filming. For instance, one day astronaut Buzz Aldrin—the man who walked on the moon— was there. He was a diver, so he asked to join us for a day of filming. I was told he was a good diver but that it was my job to keep an eye on him while I was filming. I said sure. I mean, he was Buzz Aldrin, the astronaut. I was honored. Thing is, while I was filming my shot, he kept wandering into the scene. Several times I motioned him to stay off to the side, behind me. But somehow he'd end up in my viewfinder. Finally I took him by his scuba tank and moved him out of the way, signaling, "Stay here and don't move." As soon as I'd done it, I was saying to myself, "Oh, Chuck, what have you done now? You just reprimanded a very famous astronaut." Thankfully, Buzz didn't seem to take offense and no one got onto me for it.

One of the trickiest scenes we filmed was of a shark attack. In the scene, James Bond is being towed behind the villain's boat when he gets attacked.

We used live sharks. The local Seaquarium collected them for us and we kept them in large tanks that continually circulated seawater. The thing about most sharks is that they need to swim in order to circulate enough oxygen through their gills to stay alive. Being kept in the tanks meant the sharks couldn't swim much, which caused them to be oxygen-deprived; this was actually important to us because it slowed them down enough for us to safely work with them in the scenes.

There was no way the producers were willing to risk having Roger Moore film this scene with a live eight-foot tiger shark, so Pete Romano served as his double. Pete is one of the best underwater filmmakers in Hollywood and he's also been involved in the development of underwater film equipment. He's a very capable guy and he knew just what we needed to do to get the shot.

Pete was floating on the surface with "blood bags"—plastic capsules filled with red dye—under his clothes. Al would wave, signaling the shark wrangler, a diver who was holding the shark, to shove the shark into Pete, who would start thrashing around. As Pete broke the blood bags open it looked like he'd actually been attacked—the water all around him turned dark red. It's the most realistic shark attack footage I've ever seen filmed.

It was really good. Too good, in fact. The producers ended up leaving this scene "on the cutting room floor," for fear that it would be considered too gruesome and might interfere with the film getting the right rating category for its release. This sort of thing can be frustrating for some cinematographers, but it's just part of the business.

The scene in which James Bond is being towed behind the boat—before the bloody shark attack—was also an interesting one to film. This sort of scene can usually be shot in a swimming pool with a green screen in the background, just as a close-up. But the producers wanted it filmed from a vantage point under the water, looking up from the coral reef. The viewer would see the boat from underneath, with James Bond tied to a rope, being dragged behind. To get the shot we had one of the underwater film crew kneel on the bottom, holding a big clump of coral and sea fans on top of his head so that we could get underneath and film through the coral reef for the shot. It was pretty clever filming.

That scene, while clever, was simple to pull off. Another, far more complicated scene involved filming a shipwreck, a submarine, sharks and divers all in the same frames. In *For Your Eyes Only*, two divers are in a submarine searching for a sunken ship that has an atomic bomb somewhere inside. They find the wreck and leave the sub to swim into a hole in the wreck—made by a torpedo blast—looking for the bomb. This is when a tiger shark swims out of the wreck and comes straight for them.

This scene was staged on a large cargo container that the set designers had made to look like part of a sunken ship, complete with a hole cut in the side. The hole was fashioned to look like a torpedo blast had caused the damage. When the divers emerged from the submarine and made their way toward the hole, dive crew member Terry Kirby, who was on the inside of the cargo container holding a big tiger shark, would shove the shark through the torpedo hole at the divers. Three or four other dive crewmembers were waiting on top of the container, out of the scene, and would quickly catch the shark so that we could use it for another take.

Another interesting thing about that scene is that in the film, the submersible was meant to be a dry sub. But in reality, it was a wet sub. The divers were breathing off scuba regulators that were hidden from view, and everything was set up so you couldn't tell that they were actually wet. It was a tricky scene, but we were finally ready to roll film. Al waved his arms, signaling, "action," and we started filming. Everything was going just fine until a fish worked its way inside the submarine and was swimming against the submarine's front dome. The whole thing fell apart until they could get the fish out of there. So we all just went to lunch.

Working on location together for months at a time, the crew usually becomes pretty close. We'd get together a lot after work. When we were nearing the end of our Bahamas shoot, around Christmastime, we organized a pre-wrap party at my condo. My place at the Coral Harbour had a small kitchen and a living room that had three sliding glass doors that opened to the patio. I have to admit that it was probably the first time the oven in my kitchen had been used the whole time I was there. Anyway, we had a nice party, with everyone heading home before it got too late. The set call was usually around eight o'clock in the morning, so we all needed to be up early.

I went to bed that night with the sliding doors and windows open to let the ocean breeze in. In the morning I closed the place up and took the shuttle boat to the *Moby*. I was enjoying a nap while we were waiting to be called to work when someone yelled to me that I had a call on the radio. That's when I learned there'd been an explosion in my condo. Apparently, the gas oven had a slow leak and the pilot light ignited the gas, causing the explosion.

My first question was, "Was there a fire?" Thankfully, the glass doors were blown out onto the patio, but there was no fire. The reason I was so worried about a fire was because we were paid in hundred dollar bills each week. I would put the money in envelopes and duct tape the envelopes to the wall above the curtains in my bedroom. I figured if the place got robbed nobody would think to look behind the curtains. If the explosion had caused a fire, I'd have been out nearly four months' worth of pay.

Sometimes Love
Doesn't Come Easy

In 1982 Al Giddings and I worked together on a 20th Century Fox film called *Love is Forever*, which was based on the experiences of Australian journalist John Everingham in Laos and Thailand during and after the Pathet takeover of Laos. An attractive Laotian female spy was assigned to befriend Everingham. But instead, she falls in love with him. Everingham is arrested and later exiled to Thailand. He vows to return to Laos to rescue the woman by learning how to scuba dive and swimming her across the Mekong River from Laos to Thailand.

Michael Landon was a co-producer and he also played the lead in the film, alongside Priscilla Presley, who played a scuba instructor hired to teach Everingham to dive. Despite their star power, the film was a big turkey. We had a lot of challenges getting the thing made, but Al kept reminding me that we got paid every day, no matter what.

One nice thing about the film is that my son Flip worked on it with us, as the stunt double for Michael Landon. He wore a curly gray wig for the part, which he wasn't crazy about. But he didn't seem to mind spending time scuba diving with Priscilla Presley. I did meet Michael Landon once at a production meeting. He seemed pleasant enough, but I never saw him after that.

It seems like every movie that involves underwater footage has to have the obligatory shark scene. In *Love is Forever*, which was also released as *Comeback*, we were working with a tiger shark in the Bahamas. We had the shark alongside our 14-foot Boston Whaler, towing it along to help keep it alive. That thing was bigger than our boat.

This particular job seemed to take forever. We spent a lot of time in the water—in water that was cold, murky and covered with green duckweed. We joked that the movie should be renamed *Love Takes Forever*. The duckweed got into everything—our ears, our regulators, etc. We had to construct a floating dam to keep the duckweed out.

One scene depicted Everingham being shot at while underwater. A special effects man was positioned outside the frame, shooting a 50-caliber machine gun loaded with live ammunition into the water as Flip, doubling for Michael Landon, swam past. Al and I could see them whizzing past us as we filmed. It was unnerving. Flip said a couple times he could feel the bullets hitting him, but they'd lost power pretty quickly, so they didn't harm him.

Another river-crossing scene called for Flip to get entangled in the branches of a big sunken tree, which then starts to tumble down a slope. In this scene, I was filming really close to Flip as he runs into the tree. For just a second he turns to face me, and the look on his face says, "What the hell are we doing here?!" It was priceless.

I really have to hand it to Al for keeping our spirits up and for always looking to find a solution to the problems that plagued us. For instance, he arranged to have a gas-powered hot water heater brought to the dock so we could pump hot water into our wet suits between takes. It's that kind of thinking—that kind of problem solving—that helps keep things moving along.

Another challenge we hadn't foreseen was the Florida Truckers Union. They took issue with us having our large van on the film site. The van wasn't being driven anywhere; it was set up as a staging with workbenches and shelves for our cameras. After some heated negotiations we reached an agreement with the union that a union driver would sit in the truck 24 hours a day in order to satisfy the union's requirement. The truck never moved an inch the whole time, and we ended up hiring a guy to sit in the truck with the union driver, just to make sure that all our camera equipment stayed put.

Nobody complained when we left Florida to do more filming in the Bahamas. By this time the cast and crew were all pretty good friends. I had struck up a friendship with Priscilla, and I intended to ask her out to dinner at Gray Cliffs, a nice restaurant in Nassau. Flip and I were sitting together on the back of the boat when I decided to tell him of my plans. That turned out to be a big mistake. He got up, turned to me and said, "Oh yeah?" and walked to where Priscilla was sitting on the bow of the boat and immediately asked her to go to dinner with him. He beat me to it! As it worked out, I had a lady friend who worked in Nassau so the four of us went to dinner at Gray Cliffs together.

My aim in life has always been to do my best, no matter what. I can't say that *Love is Forever* represents my best work, but I also understand that if a person is serious about his or her work, one is never really completely satisfied. I don't think there is anything I've ever done— well, maybe one photo I took of a garibaldi years ago—that I don't wish I had a chance to improve upon.

Around the World
with *Ocean Quest*

In 1985, Hollywood producer Peter Gruber and Al Giddings put together a television series for ABC, consisting of five one-hour documentary-style programs. The series, called *Ocean Quest*, starred former Miss Universe Shawn Weatherly, who as part of the series would learn how to dive and then go on a variety of exciting underwater adventures all over the world. Shawn is a wonderful woman who is as smart and capable—and kind— as she is beautiful. We spent a lot of time together during the filming and became good friends. I admire how well she handled the various challenges that came her way during the *Ocean Quest* series.

Al and I made a "recon" dive off southern California's San Clemente Island to scout a location we'd use when filming the initial sequence of Shawn's certification dives. Our maximum depth on that dive was 130 feet, which is the suggested limit for sport diving, although Al and I have routinely made dives below 200 feet for years. We followed the same dive profile, including performing a safety stop before surfacing from the dive.

Back on board the boat we quickly removed our gear and wet suits. After diving, the first thing Al would usually do is jump into a hot shower. I've always felt this is a bad idea, as it might contribute to decompression sickness. Anyway, after Al finished showering he said he felt nauseous and had some numbness. He also appeared a bit confused. We started him on oxygen and called the Coast Guard for a possible emergency air evacuation. Thankfully, within several minutes of breathing oxygen Al's symptoms subsided, so we cancelled the helicopter. It all worked out fine, but that was the end of Al's diving on this first leg of the trip.

Ocean Quest's first big international adventure had us all traveling to Australia to film Shawn Weatherly diving with great white sharks—

from safely inside a cage, of course. In the release, she appears to be very afraid to make the dive. Sharks banged against the cage as they went for the fish carcasses secured alongside. This time they weren't oxygen-deprived, half-dead sharks, but big, live, hungry ones. Shawn appears to be crying and has to be coaxed into the cage. But when she emerges, she's all smiles—thrilled to have seen great white sharks up close. People who later watched the episode on television were critical, asking why anyone would force the poor woman to get into a shark cage when she was clearly afraid. Well folks, this is why they call it "acting." Sure, Shawn was rightfully nervous about doing that first shark dive, but the tears were all for show. In fact, we actually filmed the "crying scene" after she'd already done several shark dives—and loved it! Shawn and the whole crew worked well together to make the series a success. Adding a little drama here and there was all part of the plan.

During the white shark filming we had two support boats. One was for Al and his girlfriend Rosa, Shawn and me. The rest of the film crew stayed on the other boat—the one that also carried the chum used to attract the sharks, which consisted of a bunch of bloody fish guts in giant barrels on the back deck. There really wasn't a place on that boat where you could go to escape the stench. At the end of the day Al and I would get in a 10-foot aluminum boat and row over to our boat, which was clean and fresh smelling. We'd shower and enjoy a nice dinner, without so much as a whiff of chum.

I'm fairly certain that the crew stuck aboard the stinky boat had daydreams of our little rowboat capsizing, pitching us to the great whites as we paddled away each evening.

The next *Ocean Quest* segment was filmed in the Antarctic. We flew to Christchurch New Zealand and on to McMurdo Sound on a military jet. Shawn was still an inexperienced a diver, and here we were, practically at the South Pole. She took it all in stride as we stuffed her into a bulky dry suit and shoved her through a hole in the nine foot-thick ice. The water was 27 degrees and slushy, like the consistency of a frozen margarita. She was a real trooper through it all.

Our underwater footage included images of Weddell seals and beautiful ice formations, while the topside filming illustrated the beauty of naturally formed ice caves and the struggles of surviving (and filming) in harsh conditions.

When we arrived in the Antarctic there were no ice shacks or small portable trailers available for our use, so our first dives were made out in the open, with temperatures about 50 degrees below zero. We finally were able to obtain an ice shack, which did provide a small measure of comfort as we got into and out of the water. At least it gave us shelter from the wind while we geared up. This presented a challenge for us, though, because now we faced problems with continuity. The footage wouldn't go together seamlessly. To make everything work, we ended up using the shack but also filming some sequences out in the open so the scenes would appear consistent.

Our initial shot list included the use of a hot air balloon that was shipped to Antarctica, but the conditions prevented us from using it for filming. It never flew.

We were able to use that same balloon In Truk Lagoon, Micronesia (now known as Chuuk). Since some of the World War II wrecks are visible from the air, the plan was to launch the hot air balloon from a large Navy landing craft known as an LCI, positioned in the middle of the lagoon. The open deck was perfect for maneuvering the balloon. Unfortunately, during one of the balloon launches, the balloon accidentally caught fire. The fire was quickly extinguished, but I was taking a nap atop a stack of steel scuba tanks at the time, and the commotion certainly ruined my nap.

My nap wasn't the only thing ruined as a result of the fire. During the commotion, our boat came into contact with the lagoon's most famous wreck, the *Fujikawa Maru*. It was a remarkable wreck, especially since it had one mast sticking out of the water. Our support boat hit the mast, severing it. We all were very sad that our film project impacted a historical shipwreck in such a way.

From Micronesia we made way to Australia, to dive the wreck of the *Yongala*, a famous wreck located off the central east coast. This segment included filming Shawn with venomous sea snakes and showing her with local scientists collecting the snakes, whose venom is used in medical research.

We also filmed a segment that showed Al and Shawn outfitted in chain mail "shark suits" while diving with and feeding grey reef sharks. Marine biologist Jeremiah Sullivan developed the flexible mesh suit of armor to help protect divers working with sharks. The grey reef shark is not a big shark, but is probably responsible for more shark attacks than any other shark. Not deaths, but bites. Several of my friends and colleagues have been bitten, including Jim Stewart from Scripps and Bill Curtsinger from *National Geographic*. Thankfully, both men sustained only minor injuries, but you really want to keep your wits about you when you're in the water with grey reef sharks.

I was filming Al and Shawn, wearing their protective suits surrounded by sharks, when things started getting a little exciting. There were a lot of sharks all of the sudden, and they're all darting around like crazy, looking for the speared fish that were tucked into the reef. That's when it occurred to me that here I am, right in the middle of this shark frenzy, and I'm in my BVDs and a wet suit. I'm lucky I wasn't bitten, but I also came away with some of the best shark footage I've ever filmed.

One of my favorite segments of the *Ocean Quest* series was a trip to Cuba. We dived first in the Havana Harbor searching for artifacts. The harbor was polluted, with a thick layer of oil covering the surface of the water. We came up with a few old bottles from the whaling days, and a few old coins, but no real valuable treasure. Al found a square black gin bottle that we decided was a rare find. One time while in Christchurch New Zealand, after a flight back from the Arctic, Al and I had some time and wandered into an antique store and noticed they had a few of the same rare gin bottles on display. Al talked the guy out of one for just a few dollars. He was feeling pretty smug about making such a great deal, commenting to the shop owner, "The square bottles are pretty rare, you know. They're hard to find." That's then the owner said, "If you want more of those rare bottles just let me know. I've got a whole case of them in the back." We left feeling pretty silly.

One of our crew had a Swedish girlfriend who joined us for a visit. While he was off filming a topside segment one evening, I took her and Shawn into town to find the bar where Ernest Hemingway used to hang out, the Bar La Bodequita.

Here I am on a hot Havana night, flanked by two beautiful women with long blonde hair and short white summer dresses. We walked into the bar and I immediately noticed it was full of men. No women. We asked for a table in the dining room, but the host told us there'd be a bit of a wait, so he instructed us to have a seat at the bar. It wasn't long before a man approached us and asked if he could buy us a drink. I said sure, and then he asked where we were from. When we told him we were in Cuba shooting a television series that would air in the United States, he made a very big deal, yelling to his friends that we were from Hollywood. All the sudden people were buying us drinks and we were seated in the dining room right away. We had a great time and we didn't pay for a thing. That was a memorable evening, for sure.

The trusty *Moby* once again served as our diving platform, but we also had use of Peter Gruber's beautiful motorsailer yacht, the 80-foot *Oz*. Fidel Castro paid a special visit to the marina to see the yacht and personally welcome the film crew to Cuba. When Castro approached the boat he noticed a sign that illustrated "no shoes"—a boot with a red line drawn across it. Castro stopped and began removing his boots, when Peter stepped forward and indicated that the President Castro should keep his shoes on.

Castro insisted that he didn't need any special treatment, but he did keep his shoes on. He appeared to be at ease and was very friendly with everyone, shaking our hands.

Al and Rosa, Shawn and I each had staterooms aboard the Oz, while the rest of the crew was bunking on good ol' tugboat *Moby*. The sun was setting as we made way to the north side of the island to film Cuba's blue holes. Al, Rosa, Shawn and I were sitting in the Oz's hot tub, drinking Champagne, about to enjoy a steak dinner. I just knew that the rest of the crew onboard the *Moby* would be green with envy, but I was certain they also realized that Al and I were the reason they were in Cuba, and on the *Ocean Quest* adventure.

When we finished up in Cuba we ventured to the Dominican Republic and Newfoundland to film more *Ocean Quest* episodes, but it was our wrap party when we finished filming in Cuba that I will always consider one of the greatest wrap parties of all time. On our last night in Cuba we celebrated with a lobster dinner that included gifts from Fidel Castro himself—fat, hand-rolled Cuban cigars and some of Cuba's finest rum.

Never Say Never

The next feature film Al and I worked on was *Never Say Never Again*, which was released by Warner Brothers in 1983. It was a spy film based on the James Bond novel, *Thunderball*, but because of a legal battle between the writers and producers, this film was produced as an "unofficial" Bond movie. Cubby Broccoli, whose company, Eon Productions, produced all the other films in the Bond series, was not involved.

Sean Connery reprised his role as James Bond, after a 12-year hiatus. When he'd finished filming *Diamonds Are Forever* Connery publicly declared that he would "never" play Bond again. It was Connery's wife Micheline who suggested the title, *Never Say Never Again*, referring to her husband's vow. The producers obviously liked the idea, and the title stuck.

Klaus Maria Brandauer gave a critical performance as villain Maximillian Largo, with Kim Basinger co-starring as Largo's mistress, Domino.

Al and I found ourselves working together filming in the Bahamas once more. One particular scene was staged in an underwater cave at Staniel Cay, in the Exumas. The site, known as Thunderball Grotto, has been the setting for a number of major motion pictures. It's perfect because it's in a shallow spot and at one point there's a pretty big air pocket inside. It's shallow enough that you can stand up in it. Anyway, we needed a close-up shot of Sean Connery's face, but his mask was all fogged up. Al motioned for me to fix it, so I swam Sean over to the shallow area where the air pocket was located, so we could stand up and talk. I said, "Sean, you might not like this, but give me your mask." He took the mask off and handed it to me, and I spit in it, rubbed the saliva around on the glass faceplate and then swished a little seawater inside the mask and rinsed it out. I told Sean to put the mask back on and off we went. Sean's mask stayed clear and fog-free after that. We got the close-up shot.

Later, when we were back on the boat, Sean came over and said, "Chuck I never imagined I'd thank anyone for spitting into my mask. But thank you. Your spit did the job just fine."

That's the thing about filmmaking; you just have to do whatever it takes to get the job done. And sometimes you have to improvise.

It's interesting, knowing how various parts of a film get shot in segments and then they're edited together to make the scene come to life in the finished movie. For instance, there's a scene where Sean Connery and Kim Basinger jump off a cliff into the ocean and swim to an inflatable Zodiac and climb aboard. Stunt doubles did the cliff-jumping scene, and Sean and Kim didn't actually have to swim, or even climb into the Zodiac, which was propped on the deck of the support boat. Crewmembers just sprayed them with water during the close-up. Once all the film sequences were edited together, the whole scene came together beautifully. For our crew, the most interesting part of that shot was Kim, who was wearing a sheer pink teddy.

The Happy Meal™

To work as a freelance cinematographer is to be a hired gun. Whether you're hired to shoot a major motion picture for months at a time or you just show up for the day to shoot a particular scene, you're usually there to make someone else's vision become real. Sure, it takes a certain amount of skill to get the shot, but cinematographers are sort of anonymous. You rarely get screen credits and it's not like many people outside the business know who you are.

But you're the one who knows about it when you get a paycheck.

My point is that to enjoy the life of a cinematographer, you need to be self-motivated—and also self-satisfied. You need to enjoy the work you do, to strive to be good at it and get better at it. And you need to be satisfied with the paycheck and the job well done, because it's not likely that you'll have people chasing you down the street asking for your autograph. All this has suited me just fine. It's how I've preferred it. And I guess it explains why I've enjoyed my career as a cinematographer.

I once did a McDonald's commercial just before the Los Angeles Olympics in 1984. The job was to film a sequence involving the U.S. Olympic Synchronized Swim Team. I flew to an aquatic center in LA and met with the director, who knew exactly what he wanted. He showed me the underwater camera system, asking, "Do you know how to shoot this thing?" It was just another Arriflex 35-mm camera. It even had a cable connecting it to a topside monitor that would enable the director to see exactly what I was shooting. He didn't ask for—and really didn't need—any input from me. I did the thing I was hired to do. I used my expertise with the equipment to get a clean, steady shot. And that was that. I was the guy they hired to pull the trigger.

There are times when this can be frustrating, especially when the decisions made topside aren't the best ones for a particular underwater scene. But that's the thing about being a hired gun; it pays to remember what your job is and who you're working for.

Tales from *The Abyss*

The last major motion picture that I worked on was *The Abyss*, in 1988. The science fiction and adventure film was written, produced and directed by James Cameron. It was a huge success, winning the 1990 Oscar for Best Visual Effects, Best Art Direction/Set Direction, Best Cinematography and Best Sound. Jim Cameron is the hardest working, most intelligent writer, producer, cameraman, director, editor—you name it—that I have ever been involved with. He is the whole package. A truly wonderful guy.

That said, a production as big as *The Abyss* was bound to have present a lot of challenges. That's where working with Al Giddings is a benefit, because Al always puts together a hardworking, professional crew of 12, including me as a cameraman. He built the camera systems, too.

We were originally supposed to film the underwater sequences in the Bahamas, but Cameron soon figured out that with all the special effects and stunts, he needed a controlled environment, so the production was moved to Gaffney, South Carolina, where we filmed in the abandoned Cherokee Nuclear Power Plant. One of the tanks was 55 feet deep and over 200 feet wide and held over 7 million gallons of water.

Our "home base" was a Days Inn motel in Gaffney. The Days Inn was the best place in town, which says a lot.

Most of the cast had never scuba dived before starting on this film project, so they all had to be trained and certified to dive. The gear they were using wasn't simple "recreational" scuba gear, by any stretch. They were equipped with full-face masks and heavy gear that was modified to resemble military mixed gas systems. Since so much of the filming took place underwater, James Cameron's production team designed and built a communications system that allowed him to talk underwater to the actors while allowing dialogue to be recorded directly onto tape. That was a first, and a big development in underwater comm systems for filming purposes.

When we arrived the main pool wasn't ready, and neither was the set that was being constructed in that tank. They had all sorts of problems with water filtration and clarity, and they threw a lot of different chemicals at the problem. The water didn't clear up much, but our hair turned yellow and started falling out. Crew member Rosa Chastney, who worked continuity, was wearing a pair of silver earrings and they started dissolving. We ended up taking several days off while the water issue got sorted out.

When we started work again we moved to one of the small cooling tanks that were only about 15 feet deep. A lot of time was spent just getting the cast comfortable in the heavy gear. We had all kinds of challenges getting the lighting right for the helmets, so they'd show the actors' faces.

One scene we shot in the small tank involved the divers entering a sunken atomic submarine. I was holding lighting from above actor Leo Burmeister, who played oil rig veteran, Catfish, when his full-face mask became dislodged and began flooding. He kept his cool, and I quickly dropped down to him and got my spare regulator in his mouth and got him over to the edge of the tank. He was fine, but for the next few days, when he'd see me on the set he'd thank me and tell me he owed me a few beers.

We were stuffed into the small tank for nearly two weeks before they finally got the water situation in the large tank sorted out. Now that the water was clear, the next challenge was blocking the light out so it looked like we were deep down in the ocean. Dark cloth covers got destroyed by a storm, so they ended up dumping a bunch of little black plastic beads into the water. These BB-sized beads covered the surface and blocked the light perfectly. But they also got all over us as we got out of the water—in our ears, our regulators. It was a mess.

Because the BBs turned out to be a problem it was decided that we would film at night. It meant some really long workdays, starting at 11 am and working until well after midnight, but because a few of the crew were union members, we'd never spend seven hours in the water without a meal break. After seven hours, we'd grab some food and then go sit in the Jacuzzi so we could warm up a bit. But Jim Cameron never stopped. While we took a break, he'd go work with the topside crew until we ready to get back in the water.

When filming, Jim would have a camera with a monitor where he could see exactly what each of the cameras was capturing. He would have four or five people all holding lights, waiting for his command. He would communicate to the surface and it was relayed to an underwater speaker so everyone underwater could hear him. Invariably, some poor dive crew would position a light differently than what Jim wanted, and Jim would let him have it. If you heard it, you'd have imagined that Jim was going to fire the guy as soon as they finished the scene, but then later, up on the dive deck, Jim would offer to buy the guy a cup of coffee. He never apologized—because he was always right—but he would take the time to explain why he needs everything to be done just right. He was tough to work with, but he had a way of pushing you to do your best work.

The diving helmet worn by Ed Harris in his dive to the other underwater world—the abyss—was supposedly filled with a breathable liquid. Actually, it was just filled with water. Ed Harris's stunt double, Charlie Arneson, wore special contacts and held his breath during the quick close up shots. As he is about to step off the cliff to dive into the abyss he raises his hand. It looks as if he's waving goodbye to his friends in the underwater habitat, but he's actually signaling to safety diver Terry Kirby, just out of frame, that he needs air. Terry would give him a regulator to breathe from and after Charlie took a few deep breaths he would close the helmet and hold his breath for the next shot.

The scene in which Ed Harris drops into the abyss was very challenging to shoot. To get the long moving scene Ed and Al Giddings were harnessed onto a long line with pulleys attached. They'd drop sideways about 30 feet during each take. They did this scene dozens of times over a two-day period. Both Ed and Al were very patient.

One time my job was to get footage of Jim Cameron directing the action. Rosa, Al's assistant, handled continuity on the set. As part of her job she would hit Jim's helmet with the clap board to mark the soundtrack. Over three days we shot the setup over and over again. I was to shoot Jim doing his directing—the goal was to get a close-up of his face in the helmet. I'd film it several times before needing a break. Halfway up the tank there was a ridge in the wall, so I went up there with my assistant to rest until the next setup. I was always afraid that I would fall asleep and roll off that edge with all my scuba gear and camera hanging on me, and roll into the scene. If that had happened, Jim probably would've said, "Nicklin, get on the bus!"

We spent so much time in the water at depths averaging 50 feet that the risk of decompression sickness was a real concern, so oxygen tanks were rigged with long regulator hoses staged at 20 feet so we could breathe from them while waiting for the next setup. We even had oxygen regulator hoses set up near the benches where we sat during lunch, so when we finished eating we could sit there and breathe pure oxygen.

Obviously, filming *The Abyss* was a strenuous, challenging film. It was especially tough on Al, who was accustomed to being a filmmaker, but in this instance, he was Jim Cameron's camera operator. It wasn't an easy thing for Al but I have to give him credit. He handled it well.

Photographs

Chuck's parents Mae and Charles, with a very tiny Chuck Nicklin.

Chuck's sons Terry and Flip.

Charles and Mae Nicklin.

As a young boy, Chuck enjoyed spending time with family and friends at Lake Quinsigamond in Massachusetts.

Chuck with his Navy buddies, 1945.

Chuck visits his former market—which still bears his name—located on 604 So. 38th Street in San Diego, 2012.

Chuck's favorite car, a 1936 Ford coupe.

Chuck's first Scripps c-card.

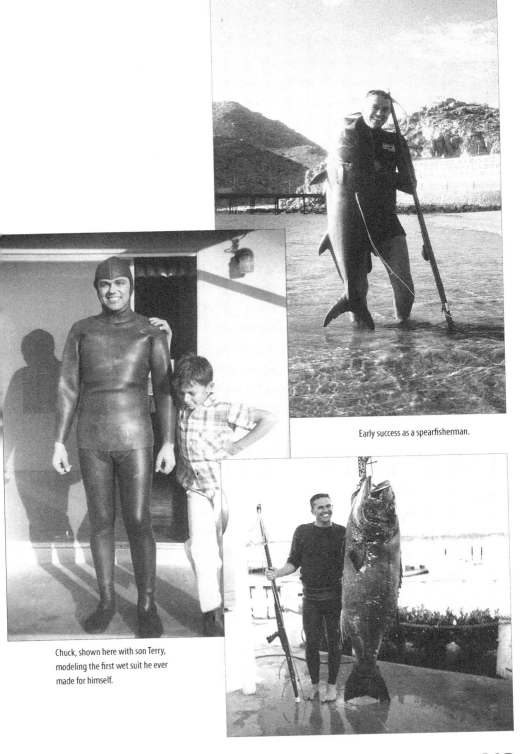

Early success as a spearfisherman.

Chuck, shown here with son Terry, modeling the first wet suit he ever made for himself.

Chuck taking underwater photos with his Rollei Marine camera.

The interior of the Diving Locker.

Flip and Chuck Nicklin with the first IMAX underwater camera—which weighed over 300 pounds—on location in the waters off Hawaii.

The Diving Locker
4825 Cass Street, San Diego.

The Diving Locker
1020 Grand Ave., San Diego.

As teenagers, Flip and Terry Nicklin were
on a team that won the Junior Pacific Coast
Spearfishing Championship.

Chuck's friend and mentor, Conrad Limbaugh.

This iconic photo of Chuck as "the man who rode a whale" was taken off La Jolla in 1963. It helped launch his career as a professional photographer.

RVICE

LUBRICATION

The DIVING LOCKER

SCUBA · GUNS · AIR · SUITS

Spearfishing figures prominently in the early history of freediving and scuba diving.

The original Diving Locker located at 4825 Cass Street in San Diego became a popular hangout for local divers.

The original Diving Locker logo.

Chuck's ability to sleep anywhere, anytime, is legendary.

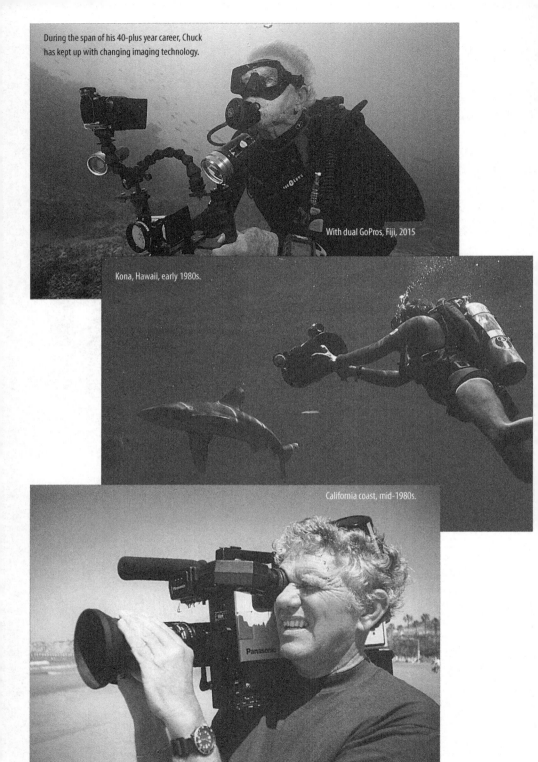

During the span of his 40-plus year career, Chuck has kept up with changing imaging technology.

With dual GoPros, Fiji, 2015

Kona, Hawaii, early 1980s.

California coast, mid-1980s.

Camera Man

Chuck filming Dr. Sylvia Earle as she makes a dive in the 1 atmosphere "Jim" suit off Hawaii.

Chuck Nicklin was inducted into the International Scuba Diving Hall of Fame in 2014.

©2014 CourtneyPlatt.com

Fiji, 2015.

149

Tahiti, early 1980s.

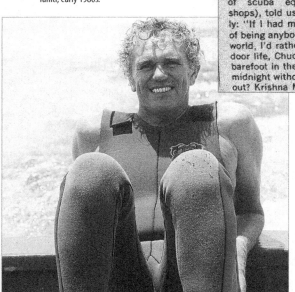

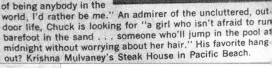

Bachelor of the Month: San Diego's Chuck Nicklin, 44, internationally known underwater photographer —he's worked with Lloyd Bridges and Jacques Cousteau— and owner of Diving Locker (California chain of scuba equipment shops), told us candidly: "If I had my choice of being anybody in the world, I'd rather be me." An admirer of the uncluttered, outdoor life, Chuck is looking for "a girl who isn't afraid to run barefoot in the sand . . . someone who'll jump in the pool at midnight without worrying about her hair." His favorite hangout? Krishna Mulvaney's Steak House in Pacific Beach.

Chuck was named "Bachelor of the Month" in a 1993 issue of *Cosmopolitan* magazine. Soon after, Mulvaney's Steak house in Pacific Beach was inundated with letters from women all over the world addressed to "Bachelor Chuck."

Wakatobi, Indonesia.

Chuck's favorite garibaldi photo,
taken in the early 1960s.

Chuck with the Panasonic Betacam.

Chuck has made it a point to keep up with advances in underwater photography and video. He enjoys rigging multiple cameras.

Tiger shark, New Providence Island, Bahamas.

Chuck in Paris after completing a *National Geographic* film project in search of the mysterious coelacanth off the east coast of Africa. Early 1970s.

Chuck's 80th birthday celebration. Palau, 2008.

Chuck's beloved 1970 Porsche 911

Chuck with the Arri Flex 16-mm camera.

Palau, 1980s.

Tiger Beach, Grand Bahama Island, 2011.

Roz and her daughter Heather created this collage of Chuck, "the man who can sleep anywhere, anytime."

Some of Chuck's dive buddies thought he was a bit nonchalant about spending long periods of time on deco stops. Chuck is shown here reading *Skin Diver* magazine and eating an apple during an extended deco stop.

Chuck and Roz Nicklin have shared many exciting adventures together, including many trips to Palau, Tonga, Indonesia, Papua New Guinea and Africa.

Chuck and Roz with underwater photographer Tony Wu.

Camera Man

Roz, daughter Heather, and Chuck on the set of *Titanic*, in Mexico. The film set was 1 7th the size of the actual ship. The film, produced by James Cameron and co-produced by Al Giddings, was released in 1997.

Roz and Chuck Nicklin on their wedding day at Sammy Ledeki's home in La Jolla, 1992.

Chuck with his mom Mae and Roz.

157

Roz's daughter, Heather Bailey.

Heather, Roz and Chuck enjoying the hot tub at their La Jolla beach house.

Camera Man

In the film, *Sharks' Treasure*, starring Cornel Wilde, eccentric charter skipper Jim Carnahan and his team of hard-luck dreamers battle sharks, bandits and their own greed to recover sunken treasure off the coast of Honduras. The film was released in 1975.

On the set of *The Deep*, with actor Robert Shaw.

Jacqueline Bisset's iconic white t-shirt.

Howard Hall worked on the set of *The Deep* as spearfisherman. He went on to have a highly successful career as an Emmy award-winning cinematographer.

The Deep, starring Robert Shaw, Jacqueline Bisset, and Nick Nolte, was released in 1977. It received Academy Award and Golden Globe nominations.

Stan Waterman, Al Giddings and Chuck Nicklin on the set of *The Deep*.

Jackie Bisset.

The Deep set, the wreck interior prior to being submerged in the film tank.

Nick Nolte relaxing between takes.

The IMAX film, *Nomads of the Deep*, released in 1979 highlighted the mysterious habits of humpback whales. Filming took place in the waters of the Red Sea, Hawaii and San Diego.

The first Circle-Vision 360° camera system built for underwater use. Originally developed by The Walt Disney Company, the system uses seven cameras arranged in a circle. The film project had Chuck traveling all over the world—from San Clemente Island to South Australia to Tahiti and Micronesia.

Chuck encounters a great white shark from the "safety" of a shark cage constructed of "chicken wire." South Australia.

"FOR YOUR EYES ONLY"

SKETCH	SCENE	
36	622-632	
ROLL	CAM.	TAKE
1021	2	10
EON		6 OCT. 80
DIRECTOR:	GIDDINGS	
CAMERAMAN:	NICKLIN	

On the underwater set of the James Bond film, *For Your Eyes Only*. Bahamas, 1980.

Underwater scenes featured in *For Your Eyes Only* included filming in a shipwreck, a submarine, and with live tiger sharks.

Camera Man

On the set of *Love is Forever*, starring Michael Landon and Priscilla Presley, 1982. Flip Nicklin was the stunt double for Michael Landon.

Flip and Chuck Nicklin filming a scene in which Michael Landon's character gets trapped underwater by a falling log.

Priscilla Presley played the part of a scuba instructor in *Love is Forever*.

Flip Nicklin and Michael Landon on the set of *Love is Forever*.

Al Giddings films a wreck in Chuuk Lagoon, Micronesia as part of the *Ocean Quest* television series.

The ABC television series *Ocean Quest* starred former Miss Universe Shawn Weatherly, who as part of the series would learn how to dive and then go on scuba diving adventures all over the world.

One *Ocean Quest* segment was filmed in the Antarctic.

Chuck with Chuuk Lagoon legend, Kimiuo Aisek.

The *Ocean Quest* crew filmed a ceremony honoring the Japanese sailors lost during World War II in Chuuk Lagoon.

Camera Man

Human remains on a Chuuk shipwreck.

Chuck with submarine pilot Don Liberatore during *Ocean Quest* filming in the Bahamas.

The *OC* crew.

171

Chuck worked as an underwater cameraman on *The Abyss* in 1988.

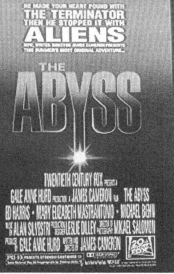

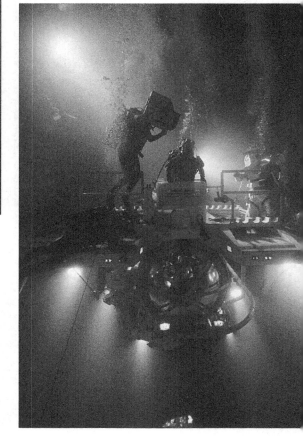

Scenes from *The Abyss* were filmed in a former nuclear power plant in South Carolina.

Chuck, right, poses with Ed Harris, left, and fellow film crewmembers.

Chuck, Sylvia Earle and Al Giddings
eating sashimi out of a scratched
Ocean Eye dome port.

Chuck with famous undersea
explorer, Jacques Cousteau.

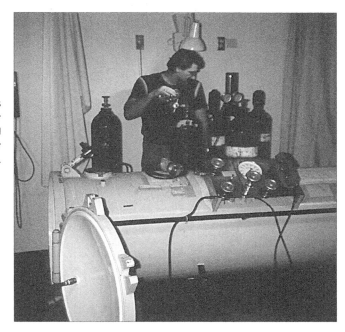

Al Giddings inspects the hyperbaric chamber inside the Chuuk hospital before being treated for decompression sickness.

Chuck with dive buddies Gordy Heck and Roger Norman.

175

Chuck with Howard Hall.

Chuck and Roz with Rocky Rockwood and Madeline Breidenbach, Fiji.

Chuck with Alan Rabbe of the *FeBrina*, Papua New Guinea.

Chuck and Roz with Harry Roushdi on the *FeBrina*.

Chuck with actor and *Sea Hunt* star Lloyd Bridges.

Chuck with Howard Rosenstein in Sharm el-Sheikh.

US Ambassador Sam Lewis, Howard Rosenstein and Chuck.

Chuck with Andy Pruna in Patagonia.

Chuck took this photo of Dr. Sylvia Earle in a Jim suit, also called an ADS (atmospheric diving suit) while on assignment for a production company. The photographer was paid a daily wage for film work and typically signed away rights to any still images produced during the assignment. The release form usually stated the photographer is to be paid one dollar for every still image. This photo became famous, and was even used in a Rolex commercial. Rolex paid for use of the image with a gold Rolex dive watch. Chuck got paid a dollar. Al Giddings got the gold Rolex.

The film *Chubasco*, released in
1967, was a big break for Chuck.

Sean Connery with
Kim Bassinger on the
set of *Never Say Never
Again*.

"Having somewhere to go is home. Having someone to love is family."

~ unknown

Thank You, Friends

When we were first putting this book together my editor, Cathryn, asked me, "What's your happiest memory about your adventures?"

That was a pretty big question. And the simple answer is, there's no one "happiest" memory. But I can tell you this: the most rewarding thing about my adventures, whether on dive trips or on film jobs or safaris or whatever, is the people I've met and the friendships I've enjoyed along the way. Some of my happiest memories are of sitting around with friends, watching the sunset and sharing stories.

When I told this to Cathryn she suggested I invite some of my friends to contribute their stories for a "guest essay section" in the book. At first I said no way—who knows what kind of wild tales my friends would come up with—but my chief editor, Roz, insisted that it'd be a good idea, so I agreed to ask a few friends if they'd be interested in sharing. The response was overwhelming.

Some friends sent stories of adventures I'd long-since forgotten, a few sent stories that reveal they are prone to exaggeration, and it seems a few people mistook me for dead and sent praise-filled stories that could serve as eulogies. Whether any of the following stories are true or not, I am honored to include them here.

Thank you, friends.

Just Don't Get in His Way

By John Binnix

I first met Chuck in 2008 on a dive trip to Fiji. I was traveling with another dive shop from Maryland, and he'd brought a group from California. I'd never heard of Chuck Nicklin.

I was relatively new to underwater photography—and not very good at it, either.

Before the first dive, several of the other divers on the boat cautioned me that Chuck was a world-class photographer and videographer and that there were several "rules" to be followed when he was shooting:

- Don't get in front of him unless he tells you to.

- Don't look at the camera unless he tells you to.

- Don't wave at the camera.

- Act natural.

- Do not get in his way.

- Be careful not to touch anything that would cause backscatter.

With all these warnings, I asked myself, "Do I even want to get in the water with this guy?"

At first I tried to stay as far away from Chuck as possible, but soon I learned that it was impossible—this guy was everywhere! It seemed like every time I turned around there was Chuck with his camera. I tried my best to stay out of the way, act natural, and not mess up the shots. I guess it worked since nobody pulled me aside and gave me a talking to after that first dive.

Well, all my fears went away after the first day of diving. Chuck turned out to be a big pussycat. I was showing some people a few of the shots I had taken, when Chuck approached and asked to see them. I have to admit, I felt intimidated. Chuck immediately put me at ease, and even gave me some pointers on how to improve my photography.

During the week we talked several times during breaks and in the evening over a few drinks and by the end of the week he was inviting me on his future trips. Since then I have had the privilege of traveling with Chuck and Roz to many exotic locations, not only for diving but also on land excursions to Africa.

I have not known Chuck for nearly as long as most of his friends have, but I consider myself lucky to have him as a mentor, and also as a great friend.

Time Well Spent

By Randi Bundschuh

From my earliest childhood memories I recall being fascinated with scuba diving from watching *Sea Hunt* episodes on television and from going with my parents to the first Diving Locker store, the one on Cass Street in Pacific Beach. I remember the place was filled with all kinds of cool stuff, and I remember Chuck Nicklin with his big smile. It seemed like it took forever for me to finally become old enough to become a scuba diver, but finally my day came.

Chuck was on board the dive boat as we made our way to a spot off Point Loma for my class's final day of scuba training. The seas were choppy and I ended up getting seasick, so the group planned to make the dive without me. That's when Chuck said he would take me on my final dive. Something about his easygoing attitude and his smile made me feel a lot less queasy and a little more confident. Suddenly I felt a whole lot better, knowing that I wouldn't be left behind and that Chuck would be diving with me. He had me geared up and in the water in no time —and off we went on my final training dive and onto many years of diving!

I made it a point to hang around the dive shop when I knew Chuck had just returned from one of his trips just so I could ask him about the exotic places he had visited and the adventures he'd had. It was time well spent. His stories inspired me to have that kind of life, too.

And I did. On several occasions I was able to join Chuck on trips where I had the chance to watch him film underwater. No matter what, Chuck is always happy to spend time helping other aspiring underwater photographers and filmmakers get better results. When he travels he always shows the highest respect for the people and the places he visits, and he helps the guests on his trips appreciate experiencing and learning about other cultures and how to respect them.

I know I am one of many people who consider themselves fortunate to know Chuck and to have learned from him—and to call him a friend.

Chuck Nicklin's Filming Tips

Keep the camera steady. This is the most important thing—it's what separates the professional camera people from the picture takers.

Control your buoyancy. Disturbing the bottom not only creates bad visibility for your film, but also can damage sea life.

Aim your lights at an angle to lessen backscatter.

Keep your zooming to a minimum.

Mix it up. The most common error is to shoot all wide-angle scenes. This is easy, but will not give a professional looking edit. Start with a wide shot to establish the scene, and then be sure to get a medium shot before moving in for a close-up. Shoot extreme close-ups and cutaways to hold attention and to allow edit moves.

Concentrate on short scenes, but don't be afraid to start the action early. No matter how much you love the shot, it won't work if it starts in the middle of the action.

Shoot action coming toward the camera, not moving away.

The scene must be in focus or it's useless.

On *The Deep* and In the Deep With Chuck

By David Doubilet

On *The Deep*

In 1976 I worked on the motion picture The Deep with Chuck. We stayed on Peter Island in the British Virgin Islands next to the famous shipwreck, the RMS Rhone. We contrived a band, with me on the banjo and Chuck rhythmically opening and shutting the valve on a scuba tank.

We shot interior wreck scenes in Bermuda in a giant studio tank scooped out of a hillside. The tank was fabulous; it was over 30 feet deep, populated with fish, ancient canons and a giant moray eel. We even had a few sharks in the tank. Every shot had three underwater cameras constantly rolling. Al Giddings, underwater director was on camera one, Stan Waterman was behind camera two and Chuck manned camera three. Scene after scene, Chuck came up with the prized footage. He was smooth and calm, his footage perfectly exposed, perfectly composed.

Chuck Nicklin above else is a cameraman. Moving a motion picture camera (now a video camera) is and always will be an art. It is a visual dance felt with your body and interpreted through your eyes. It must be smooth and precise. It must elegantly capture moments that draw you into the story like moths to a flame. This is Chuck Nicklin.

In the Deep

In 1978 Chuck and I worked on a *National Geographic* story on Hawaii's precious coral with coral biologist and legendary surfer Dr. Ricky

Grigg. We dove with the black coral divers of Maui as they harvested the corals out of the deep waters in the Auau Channel between Maui and Lanai. At any given moment most of the Pacific pours through the Auau Channel.

Our dive plan was simple: each of us would carry an Ocean Eye housing as we followed behind the coral divers wearing double tanks on Hawaiian backpacks. They suited up in wet suits long missing knees or elbows and rolled three rubber body bags up with 50 feet of nylon cord and a snap clip tucked into their weight belts. Each diver also carried a 16-pound sledgehammer tucked into his belt. Chuck and I decided this was idiotic, when a smaller, lighter hammer would do the job of harvesting black coral.

I remember Chuck looking over at me, saying, "David, take slow, *deeeeeep* breaths before we roll."

The bottom was 220 feet below and we were on the most absurd drift dive. The coral divers dropped like bombs through the clear water as Chuck and I kicked and pushed the big Ocean Eye housings downward, realizing our mistake as we struggled for every foot.

At 100 feet we finally saw the bottom, a blue rolling plain dotted with black coral trees. We finally reach the bottom, rolling in the current. I was out of breath and dizzy as I began to shoot—or at least I thought I was shooting. Nitrogen and carbon dioxide build-up began to take its toll. My head was pounding and I felt dizzy. Just as I was about to pass out Chuck grabbed the valve on my Fenzi and cracked it open. We rose slowly at first, and then like a rocket, with Chuck hanging on my fins to slow my ascent.

As we decompressed we watched as the coral divers sent the coral up, the body bags serving as lift bags. We climbed into the boat weary from our self-induced drama. One of the divers casually rolled a joint the size of a submarine sandwich.

Camera Man

The next day Chuck arrived better prepared for the day's dives—each with our own 16-pound sledgehammers. This time we dropped like bombs. We dove with the coral divers for two weeks. I offered to pay for gas and expenses but they said "Naggghh, just throw us a small party." They chose a nice French restaurant and showed up with wives, girlfriends, and an entourage of friends. Chuck commented on how nice it'd be to spend a quiet evening sharing a few bottles of wine among friends.

Hours later I got the bill, which included a five-course meal and six cases of rare, vintage French wine. Chuck wisely said, "David, you should have paid for the gas."

Career Advice from Chuck

By Howard Hall

In 1976 I was a twenty-six year old diving instructor working in Chuck Nicklin's San Diego Diving Locker. I was a moderately good spearfisherman and a budding underwater still photographer. Chuck had much to do with my initial pursuits in the latter. It is unlikely I would have achieved any significant measure of success as an underwater photographer without Chuck's help and inspiration.

For example: In the back room of the Diving Locker, there was a small closet. Inside, Chuck kept his photographic equipment. Not only was this closet unlocked, but Chuck allowed his goofy assortment of snorkel salesmen to use his gear as they wished. Chuck's only admonition was that the gear be returned to the closet in better condition than when it left. This was sometimes difficult to do. Loaning his precious camera gear to wannabes just becoming familiar with the functionality of o-rings was, of course, insane. But we worshiped him for it. I captured my first underwater images using Chuck's Nikonos II camera.

I was not the only wannabe that Chuck stimulated. There were many, and a significant number went on to stellar careers in diving and underwater imaging. Chuck's lifestyle was narcotically inspirational. Chuck owned the most successful dive shop in San Diego. He employed talented managers, so he didn't seem to work very hard. He drove a Porsche. He had a new girlfriend every month—each more beautiful than the last. And he regularly traveled to far-off, exotic places as a bachelor underwater cameraman for hire. *Sea Hunt*'s Mike Nelson had a somnolent lifestyle in comparison. Chuck often warned his enraptured flock that underwater photography could not be considered a serious career. That without regular income from the Diving Locker he could not survive on camera assignments alone. That careers in banking, education, or retail management were much more mature. Then he would slip into his dark blue Porsche next to a stunning model and speed off to dinner at the Chart House. Banking! Seriously?

Chuck initiated my first major break in the underwater film business. He'd been hired to film underwater scenes for Peter Benchley's motion picture, *The Deep*. A shark sequence was to be produced in the Coral Sea. The underwater film crew would be populated with diving luminaries including Al Giddings, Stan Waterman, Jack McKenney, and others. They needed a spearfisherman to help attract and incite sharks. I suspect prerequisites included experience with a speargun, unrealistic ambition, and no more than average IQ. Chuck asked me if I wanted the job as we walked down Grand Avenue to lunch one day. I considered the offer for less than a millisecond. Not only would I meet underwater filmmakers whose careers were stratospherical, I would be diving with them!

Months later, my enthusiasm peaked when I met these heroes at LAX for the 14-hour flight to Australia, and took my seat tightly sandwiched between Stan Waterman and stuntman, Howard Curtis. After ten hours or so, my glee had faded a bit, but not by much.

Eventually, we arrived in Townsville, Australia where we loaded up the first Australian live-aboard, *Coralita*, for the 30-hour crossing to the atolls of the Coral Sea. The wind was blowing a steady 30 knots and *Coralita*'s captain said we should wait. But Giddings was having none of that. He had a deadline and it would not wait. Ten hours later my enthusiastic glow had dimmed much further as I slid back and forth across the deck in *Coralita*'s salon, occasionally impacting Jack, Howard, and still photographer, Peter Lake, while I desperately trying to avoid puking all over myself and my new acquaintances. Before arriving at Marion Reef, I had vowed that if only the damn boat would stop rolling I would take Chuck's banking suggestion to heart. In fact, I had promised our good Lord to give up diving entirely and dedicate my life to altruistic works if He would only stop the *Coralita* from pitching and heaving. Chuck was not seen during this hellish trip except to stagger into the galley in search of the occasional snack before returning to the floor of his cabin. As those who read this book will certainly learn, Chuck has a talent for sleeping anywhere, anytime, and through anything.

As *Coralita* pulled through the pass into the lagoon at Marion Reef my outlook on life changed dramatically. Suddenly, the water was calm, the sun was out, people were standing up without being thrown into a bulkhead and I was, once again, the happiest guy on the planet. I immediately rescinded the vow to my Maker.

For three weeks our crew filmed sharks in the Coral Sea. We had many memorable adventures during the expedition, one that included two 50-gallon drums full of cattle blood that nearly exploded due to fermentation in the tropical sun. Perhaps Chuck will remember that unfortunate olfactory experience. But one of the dives we made in the Coral Sea together will certainly remain memorable for both of us. It is the single time I ever witnessed what can only be described as a shark feeding frenzy.

Our crew was on the bottom 110 feet below *Coralita*. Al had positioned a mock-up of a ship's hatch cover and a suction dredge on the sand 30 feet from the edge of the reef. Doubling for Robert Shaw, Howard Curtis was to descend wearing a surface-supplied Desco diving mask. Chunks of fish had been tied to the hose. Appropriately, Howard would not be relying on the surface supplied air since we intended that sharks tear the hose apart. Instead, he would be connected to a pair of tanks via a 20-foot long low-pressure hose once he reached the bottom. This part of the plan didn't work out very well because sharks tore the hose apart only moments after Howard entered the water. Eventually, Howard did make it down carrying the pair of tanks under his arm.

The plan was quickly modified. Al, Stan, and Chuck would concentrate on sharks threatening Howard and would avoid shots of the severed hose above his head. With Howard standing on the hatch cover and the cameramen taking shelter against the coral reef, it was time for me to earn my pay. Al signaled to me by pointing his finger and cocking his thumb. "Shoot something," was the signal. I was a bit reticent. Looking up, the sky was filled with gray reef sharks.

Just beyond Howard Curtis and the dredge, there was a small clump of dead coral resting on the sand. Hovering above this limestone rock was a lovely little seaperch just over a foot long. I swam toward it rather hoping it would swim away. I realized that 60 or more sharks competing for one mortally injured little seaperch might produce a rather precarious situation. Hoping for a reprieve, I looked back over my shoulder at the film crew. Al gave the "shoot" signal again with an amplification that seemed to say, "What the hell's the matter with you? Shoot, damn it. Shoot!" I took aim then looked up at the cloud of sharks one more time giving the fish a final chance of escape. Then I fired.

The seaperch was impaled halfway up the spear shaft. I didn't like the idea of it swimming to take shelter under my arm. So I shoved the gun away from me. Two feet from my hand, the spear gun was hit by three or more sharks and torn apart. A ball of sharks instantly formed and rumbled across the bottom creating a sound like an earthquake. Chuck, Al, and Stan rolled their cameras as Howard Curtis kicked at sharks that broke away from the roaring ball. I made it to the reef and hid behind Stan Waterman. A shark darted past me and ran into Stan from behind, knocking his forehead into his camera. He turned to see me standing there and he looked at me as if saying, "Why the hell did you do that?"

Once the action died down and the crew began their ascent, I swam out over the sand and retrieved the remains of my spear gun. Back aboard *Coralita*, Jack laid the pieces of the gun on the deck and began taking photographs of the remains. Chuck sidled up to me and said quietly, "You know Howard, no film is worth getting bit for." This was not the sort of advice you take very seriously or consider very long before accepting. But I do remember those words. It was the sort of thing you remember when you are just starting out on a long journey. Chuck Nicklin was at the peak of his career. And thanks to Chuck, I was just beginning mine.

The Professional and the Predator

By Eric Hanauer

In 1984 I was just getting started as a published writer and photographer. Having spent three months that summer in the Red Sea, I decided to enter a slide show in the San Diego Film Festival. At that time it was the premiere event of its kind, attracting some 3,000 people each of two nights. It consisted primarily of slide shows, with a few celebrity films interspersed. Slide shows were the jealously guarded purview of members of the San Diego Underwater Photographic Society, so when I showed up as a carpetbagger from Orange County, I felt about as welcome as Hillary Clinton at a Tea Party convention. I didn't know Chuck at the time, except for his reputation. Yet when I ran my show for the judges, he walked up and said, "That was one of the best shows we've had here in a long time."

Egos can run large in the world of underwater filmmaking, but Chuck appears immune. Despite all his accomplishments, he remains easygoing, and a true professional.

Except for that one time when we were at Holbox Island, off Mexico's Yucatan peninsula to film the aggregation of whale sharks. This was before the dive community discovered the Isla Mujeres aggregation, so Holbox was the only game in town for guaranteed whale shark encounters. The drawback, as in most whale shark aggregations before Isla, was green-tinted water and about 20-foot visibility, which doesn't exactly cut it when trying to film 30-foot whale sharks. The trick was to spot the fin on the surface at a distance, then swim to where you think the animal is headed, hoping it continues to come your way. I was doing exactly that, and through my viewfinder saw the dim image of a whale shark's head. Suddenly I was shoved aside, and all I could see was a set of dive fins splashing in front of my face. It was Chuck, going after the shot.

Chuck is one of the nicest, gentlest people I know, but when his shooter instinct clicks in, he's a predator.

I count myself in a long list of Chuck's protégés. He convinced me to start shooting video just before the magazine business and the market for still photography began their precipitous decline. Since then I'm shooting about 75 percent video, and have even made a few dollars doing it.

As an aging "senior" diver, I often wonder how much longer I'll be able to follow this frivolous pursuit. But then I look at Chuck and realize I've still got a few years left. He's my role model.

Taking Time, Capturing Time

By Francine Hebert

"**H**ow'd he get that shot?" was always something I wondered when I looked at Chuck's photos. I first met Chuck on a dive trip to Australia's Great Barrier Reef. While I had been diving for a while by that time, I had not yet taken up underwater photography. After our return from that trip, Chuck shared some photos he'd taken, and the colors and details he'd captured caught my eye and sparked my fascination for photography. His enthusiasm was contagious and it didn't take long for me to be among many others that were inspired by his work and want to join the ranks of amateur underwater photographers trying to give a peek of the beauty and colors of the world beneath the sea to my nondiving friends and family.

I not only admire Chuck for his work, but also for the person that he is, especially for his willingness to share his talent. He will always take time to encourage a fellow diver and photographer, whether it's a total amateur shooter or a fellow award-winning cinematographer like himself. I started out, as many of us did in the early 1970s, with a Nikonos II with macro extension tubes that increased the odds that I would get at least some photos in focus. With Chuck's guidance and encouragement I soon moved to a Nikon SLR camera in a metal housing with a strobe light and that's when I really started wondering how he got the shots he did because mine just didn't look like his. His photos told a story and while I may have seen the subject of his photos many times on my dives, they never stood still and posed for me like they seemed to for him.

He always gives willingly of his time and talent to anyone starting out and interested in underwater photography. There are a couple of things he said during those early years that have always stuck with me. They were to keep shooting—shoot a lot of photos and not to be so quick to throw out the slightly out of focus ones because sometimes if it's a rare subject it's worth keeping even if the image isn't technically perfect.

I'm not sure that he was aware at the time how profoundly true those words would be in just a few short years. Looking back at some of the photos Chuck took on the WWII wrecks of Truk Lagoon in Micronesia in the 1970s for example and then seeing photos of the same ships just a few years later would show the changes that have taken place in those waters over time. Many of the artifacts that he photographed are no longer on the ships and the coral and fish are not as abundant as they once were. I'm sure the same is true in for a lot of places that Chuck has filmed. His photos are chronicling the changes—capturing time in some of our favorite dive spots.

From Competition to Collaboration

By Werner Kurn

I first came from Germany to America as a foreign exchange student. I grew up with a love of the outdoors, hiking and skiing in the mountains, and I immediately fell in love with the California coast. Like so many others, I got my scuba training at the Diving Locker and it seems like I was in the dive shop every other day, getting tanks filled. I was passionate about diving and dreamed of one day owning my own dive store.

My wife Myra and I opened our dive store, Ocean Enterprises, in 1979. By that time the Diving Locker—one of the premier San Diego dive shops—had been open for decades. Both Chuck Nicklin and the Diving Locker had sterling reputations. It's fair to say that Chuck and I were business competitors, but as the sport grew, so did all of our businesses. There was plenty enough to go around.

For about the next 25 years or so, I envisioned a merger between the Diving Locker, which now had several locations, and our growing number of Ocean Enterprises dive centers. About once or twice a year I'd phone Chuck's son Terry Nicklin, who managed the Diving Locker, and invite him and Chuck to lunch to see if we might discuss the prospect of joining forces. Terry was always polite, but his answer always the same, "My dad says why should we have lunch with some German guy who wants to take away our business?" We never met for lunch.

Then Chuck's wife Roz entered the picture. Roz and my wife Myra had met, and liked each other. It was Roz who asked Terry and Chuck, "Why wouldn't you want to meet with some guy who might be interested in partnering with you, or buying the Diving Locker? I think you should meet him. I like his wife."

Chuck ended up selling his Diving Locker stores to others, but through the feminine wiles of our wives, we finally did meet. And we all became really good friends. In fact, after Chuck "retired" he and Roz came to work with us at Ocean Enterprises, leading dive trips and even a few safaris. He and Roz proved to be a great addition to the Ocean Enterprises team, and our friendship has grown. I have a great deal of respect and admiration for them.

I share this story not to beat Chuck up for refusing to have lunch with me way back when, or for viewing me as the competition instead of a potential collaborator, but to praise his wife Roz for bringing out Chuck's softer side. Roz is a wonderful woman. And together, they're a great couple. Chuck has often said that marrying Roz was one of the best things he ever did.

I think he's right.

On Capturing the Story and Keeping Up with Technology

By Lance Milbrand

I was working as a boat bottom cleaner, day after day, daydreaming underwater of something more rewarding, something more fulfilling than just scraping boat hulls and collecting a paycheck. Every few days I would bring my empty tanks in to the dive shop to get them filled. I got to know the employees of The Diving Locker but the owner was never in; he was always out working, shooting a film in some exotic location. And then one day the guy that helped me unload my tanks and carry them in to get filled turns out to be the shop owner. It was cameraman Chuck Nicklin—and because of that chance meeting my life would never be the same.

Chuck is a man with charisma, a huge smile and a firm handshake. It was the early 1980s and there were only a handful of successful underwater cinematographers out there and Chuck was one of them. I was in my twenties and hanging out at the dive shop was a natural extension of my life but after meeting Chuck I had another reason to visit. Could there be a future for me in cinematography? I had to explore this field.

The Diving Locker was just starting to offer dive travel and I joined Chuck on an expedition to Loreto, Mexico where we took day trips on a few panga dive boats. Up until this time, traveling divers were shooting with still cameras. Chuck helped change the way trips were planned by introducing video dive trips. I will never forget swimming next to Chuck as he discovered a pufferfish hovering over a coral head. He captured the wide shot, slowly approached, shot its face and profile. As the fish turned and swam away he followed it inches from its tail and then stopped, letting the puffer swim off. Watching that scene unfold was underwater storytelling, in-camera sequence building. This was no longer a hobby for me. I was hooked.

More trips followed, with us hauling our Hi8 rigs to Cozumel. Then Chuck organized the first dive trip to Cocos Island, Costa Rica. It was 1989 and before the *Undersea Hunter* live-aboard began exploring the region. Knowing that I had wanted to learn more, Chuck and his friends Joe Thompson, Ozzie and Dottie Wissell encouraged me to shoot 16-mm movie film. It was an expensive learning curve but learning by doing has its advantages because I had great mentors. My Cocos Island film would later premier at the San Diego Underwater Photographic Society's annual film festival where Chuck was a founding member.

Naturally, companies called Chuck all the time about working on their movie projects and he would go off and work on jobs. One time he hired me to assist him in Monterey and we worked on a film for the BBC Blue Peter, a children's series. When Chuck was on extended jobs he would send me post cards and sometimes photos. One of the jobs that took him away was the feature film, *The Abyss*, with cameraman Al Giddings and director James Cameron. I cleaned boat bottoms in envy and realized that a young cameraperson's career is a series of ups and downs. Chuck had it all figured out because even when he did not have a cameraman job, he had a steady income from owning The Diving Locker.

The takeaway from this experience is that Chuck Nicklin had a big influence on my early career. Cameras have changed tremendously in the past 35 years. Transitioning from 16-mm film to Super 16-mm film, three-quarter-inch to Betacam to Digi Beta, from Hi8 to HDV, Full HD, 4K and now 8K. I look back at my humble career and understand that one has to create their own destiny in this crazy business—and keep learning the formats or be left behind. Chuck the cameraman has done very well for himself and I feel fortunate to have him as a friend and mentor. It changed my life.

Camera Man

Simple Lessons

By Blake Miller

The first time I met Chuck was on an SSI (Scuba Schools International) shoot at Harbor Island, Bahamas in about 1986. I felt an immediate connection with him. Maybe it's because cameramen tend to see the world a little differently. Harbor Island was our first trip working together and I was a young diver, just getting my start. Chuck was a veteran, built from the salt of the sea with an ocean of stories and wild adventures in his wake. He had the hair, beard and gritty smile of King Neptune. He was a large presence, but friendly and welcoming, with a wealth of knowledge. Chuck became the greatest mentor in my life. Here are a few lessons he taught me.

LESSON 1 – How to speak "Chuck." Filming training videos, Chuck and I would spend a few weeks together on location—tough assignments on islands with beaches and water straight out of a Corona commercial. In reality, we spent more time working underwater than relaxing topside. Filming, surrounded by colorful marine life, and focused intensely on our jobs, it was easy to lose track of time. We would do many dives each day. Between dives we would check our shot list, switch out tanks, plan our next dive and brief the crew. Then we would do it all again.

The final dive of the day was always the best. Chuck would make a fist with his thumb and pinky extended like a Hawaiian "hang loose" symbol, and then bring it to his mouth like a bottle of beer. I always enjoyed when Chuck gave this hand signal for "time to eat and drink." I'd break into a smile every time, water leaking into my mask as I did so. It meant the end of the day and a job well done. I still use the "Chuck" signal and recommend it for every diver.

LESSON 2 – It's not the size of your lens, but how you use it. It's not like a man to take pride in how small his gear is, but Chuck always did.

The mini DVD tapes he filmed with years ago were tiny compared to the huge Betacam tapes I used. Flying home after a shoot, I would struggle hauling my big box of tapes home through the airport, Chuck would stroll along with his small box of mini DVD tapes, grinning and joking and asking why I used such big tapes.

Chuck taught me that great footage is captured through great composition, timing, knowledge—and sometimes a little luck. More important than the size of your gear is the artistic freedom your gear allows. This is the great thing about Chuck. He knows filming underwater has a lot of variables, and sometimes simpler is better.

LESSON 3 – How to dive with style. When I first witnessed Chuck's amazing dive skills, we were in the Bahamas again, around 1990. We were creating SSI's Open Water Diver training videos, the first in the industry. We had a fantastic trip working and filming every day, watching dailies and relaxing when we could. Near the end of the trip we had a rare chance to make a "fun" dive without our cameras.

I was diving along a coral head looking at the gorgeous colors, when suddenly, swimming on the other side, was Chuck, smiling. Then it occurred to me that the reason I noticed his smile is because he didn't have a regulator in his mouth. He was freediving. I looked at my gauge. It read 66 feet. Chuck was casually swimming along enjoying the reef. Witnessing one of the great dive pioneers in action that day was as amazing as the beautiful reef. This was diving with style.

LESSON 4 – If you lose you won't snooze. At the beginning of a shoot, we arrived at Catalina Island, and as we checked into our rooms, Chuck was bunking with a photographer friend, Greg Ochocki. I was in the hallway when the two walked into their room. Through the doorway, I could see the room only had one bed.

Without hesitation, Chuck tossed his suitcase from several feet away and it landed right in the middle of the bed. Turning to his roommate he said, "I know where I'm sleeping." We all broke into laughter, although Greg may not have laughed quite as hard as Chuck and I did. To this day I use Chuck's bag-toss technique whenever checking into a room on a film shoot—partly for good luck, partly for good sleep.

LESSON 5 – Don't try and keep up with Chuck. Chuck and our SSI crew traveled to St. Lucia together around 1995 or 1996 for a three-week shoot. At the time, Chuck was in his late 60s. One afternoon, we were filming divers swimming between coral heads quite a distance from shore. Without warning, Chuck shot off like a cannon, kicking to the surface and swimming like a torpedo towards the beach. Concerned, technical director, Dennis Pulley and I chased after him.

It turns out the alarm in his housing had gone off, indicating a water leak. Luckily Chuck's new camera was still dry—the alarm was a "false alarm."

LESSON 6 – This ocean ain't big enough for both of us. Filmmakers and still shooters often work together, although they shouldn't. Underwater still photographers like to snap on their wide-angle lenses, swim super-close to the action, and fire off their strobe flash. For a motion cameraman filming in the same waters, this is maddening. The still photographer is always right in the shot, and if he's not, the flash from his strobe is ruining it.

After one dive, a still photographer once asked Chuck, "Was I too close?" Chuck replied, "If you're in the same ocean, you're too close." I agree.

It is always a blessing to spend time with Chuck. A few years ago, I had the opportunity to go to San Diego and visit him and his beautiful wife, Roz. They live the best life. During the trip, I filmed Chuck for a series I created for Outside Television called *Image Quest*. These segments tell the behind-the-scenes stories of professional photographers and filmmakers. Chuck's story is fantastic, so check it out online if you have a chance.

A Tale of *Botos* and Busted Gear

By Greg Ochocki

In the summer of 1993 I traveled with Chuck Nicklin to the remote jungle rivers of Brazil in search of the strange and mysterious *boto*, the Amazon River dolphin, *Inia geoffrensis*.

Also known as the pink river dolphin, the *boto* is a large freshwater dolphin found in the Amazon and Orinoco Rivers and their tributaries. Known to forage in flooded forests during the rainy seasons, they grow to about five- to seven-feet long and get their name from their grayish to pinkish coloration.

Chuck was shooting footage for Oxford Scientific Films. The National Geographic Society secured special work visas on our behalf, as the video footage would ultimately appear on a National Geographic Society television program.

Chuck and I flew to Rio de Janeiro for some initial meetings about the expedition before traveling to the city of Manaus, on the Amazon River, where we secured the services of a local guide to take us deep into the blackwater tributaries.

Our guide arrived in a 20-foot open boat, called a panga, which was barely more than a dugout canoe with a sketchy outboard engine strapped to it. I wondered aloud, "Is this the panga that will take us to the bigger boat?" At this point Chuck laughed and said, "Greg, I fear this *is* our boat."

He was right.

I don't know how we managed it, but the four of us—me, Chuck, our guide, and the young boy who ran the boat—squeezed into this tiny little boat, now fully loaded with piles of expensive camera gear. The gunnel was only inches above the waterline. I feared that if I sneezed I might sink the thing.

We survived the boat ride, but photographing the elusive *botos* proved daunting. The dolphins would surface for just a few seconds before disappearing into the murky water. Our frustration mounted as the day wore on. By sunset, we were exhausted. Chuck finally said to our guide, "Well, it'll be dark soon, so I think we better call it a day. How far are we from the place where we'll be staying?"

The guide stared blankly at Chuck. Here we are, deep in the Amazon jungle and this guy hadn't thought to arrange any place for us to stay? Darkness was upon us—and with the dark came swarms of blood-sucking bugs.

We ultimately rented space in the bunkhouse of a cattle ranch not too far up the river. It wasn't the Hilton, but at least we had a place to hang our hammocks at night. The temperature inside the bunkhouse must have been over 100 degrees, but that gave us a little bit of protection from the bugs. And best of all, they had cold beer.

After three days of shooting, Chuck's footage was disappointing. The water was so murky and the *botos* were very skittish. It was pointless to continue, so we flew to Bella Horizonte. Located there was a small research facility on the shores of Lago de Plata, home to two Amazon River dolphins, a male and a female.

Things were looking up. That is, until Chuck began assembling his underwater video housing and one of the two stainless spring clips that clamp the underwater housing together broke into pieces. Chuck sat there, staring at the floor. I knew what he was thinking—it would take weeks to get one shipped to Brazil and maybe even longer to get it cleared through customs.

Camera Man

I'm known for overpacking and I've been teased for it a time or two. This time my habit saved the day. I reached into my overstuffed suitcase and pulled out a shiny new clip—the same kind I used for my Nikon still camera—and tossed it to Chuck.

Over the next few days Chuck got exactly what he needed. The conditions in the smaller lake were perfect and he got brilliant footage of the magnificent *botos*. The footage appeared later that year in a program on National Geographic Explorer TV.

"Thanks for your help."

By Liz Parkinson

knew the shots he wanted to get, I just had to be patient and wait for the perfect lineup. There had been many opportunities over the last few days, but my partner kept turning at the last minute or gliding up and over the lineup. Chuck Nicklin had brought a group of divers from California to experience one of the best 20-foot scuba dives in the world. Tiger Beach is found 27 miles north of West End, Grand Bahama, where the Great Bahama bank comes to an end, sloping down into the deep waters of the Atlantic Ocean. This area is home to a large population of tiger sharks and was the location of our weeklong dive trip. Freediving rather than on scuba, I was floating on the surface waiting for my partner—a 14-foot female tiger shark to swim below me so that the line of photographers, up current of me, might be able to capture the moment. This can sometimes be a long process but there really was no point in getting frustrated. You just have to concentrate on your positioning, stay focused and enjoy the process. I must say it was hard not to do on this day. I was in one of my favorite places, doing what I love, among a group of people whose range of talent has brought the underwater world alive through many years of photography and videography.

I kept glancing down trying to catch "the nod" from Chuck, indicating that I should prepare to dive. I looked at the bottom and saw the shark. It really is an incredible experience; swimming along side such a beautiful animal.

Finally, I got the nod. I took a slow, deep breath and went for it, and with a few kicks I found myself descending onto the back of the tiger shark, adrenaline rushing through me as I swam atop and alongside her. I gauged the scene through the mirror image projected on Chuck's dome port, kicking hard to keep up with the shark, but also trying to hold the calm composure that makes a scene like this one look magical, otherworldly. And effortless.

Chuck is a total pro. We got the shot. I felt honored to work with Chuck. And lucky that he'd even get in the water with me, after the way our initial meeting went.

You see, I was leading a dive one morning at Stuart Cove's Dive Bahamas when I first met Chuck Nicklin and his lovely wife Roz. We were on the southeastern side of New Providence at the popular "James Bond" wrecks—where underwater scenes for the classic "007" movies had been filmed decades ago. I'd just given a dive briefing to the dozen or so divers and most of them were busy getting geared up and entering the water. Except for this "slightly older" (said affectionately) couple sitting up at the front of the boat. I immediately sensed that they must be new to diving and decided they might need a little more time to get prepared for the dive. So, as any responsible dive guide would do, I took a seat next to them and set out to make them feel at ease. I launched into a lengthy description of the dive site and the safety procedures for the dive, including being good buddies and monitoring their gauges and making a slow ascent and doing a safety stop. And so on. I continued with a detailed description of the dive site, the lay out of the wrecks, their history and a bit of trivia on the two Bond movies that were filmed here. I was on a roll. After we did a thorough check of their gear and I had discussed the importance of mask defog, I felt that they were ready to make the dive. Before he stuck his regulator in his mouth, the older gentleman smiled and said, "Thanks for your help. You know Liz, when I was here in 1980 filming *Never Say Never Again*, I never thought these wrecks would become such a huge tourist attraction. Stuart really has done a great job."

With that he slide into the water, turned and asked the captain to hand him his camera. Roz joined him, and off they went. The captain chuckled to himself while I stood silent, my mouth open, my face flushed red.

Camera Man

Even though I felt embarrassed, Chuck and Roz were gracious and kind. Over the years I have been privileged to work with them, and they've taught me a lot. I cherish our times together. And Chuck's video of me swimming with the tiger sharks that day stands out as one of my favorites.

"We're here to have fun."

By Shirley Pomponi

I had the good fortune of meeting Chuck and Roz through our mutual friend Al Giddings. Many of the good times my husband Don Liberatore and I have had with Chuck and Roz have been at Al's ranch in Montana.

My favorite "Chuck Story" happened when we were traveling together in the Solomon Islands. It was our first live-aboard dive trip, 19 of us on the *Bilikiki*. We weren't certain what was in store, but we knew we'd have fun diving with Chuck and Roz. On the first night, the captain (whose name I can't remember, but I'm sure Chuck will) gave us a thorough orientation. There would be an early breakfast, a dive at 08:00, with hot showers, warm towels and cookies following the dive; another dive at 11:00—followed by hot showers, warm towels, and lunch. Then another dive at 13:00, followed by—yep, you got it—hot showers, warm towels, and this time—snacks and popcorn. There would be another dive at 16:00, followed by the fourth hot shower and warm towels, appetizers, cocktails (if you weren't making the night dive), and dinner. And for the adventurous, a night dive at 20:00. Whew! Don and I exchanged wary glances. What had we signed up for?

When the captain finished his briefing, Chuck stood up, smiling, and said, "You're all here on vacation. We're here to have fun. Dive as little or as much as you like!" I could've kissed him! Of course, we were all up early the next morning for breakfast, and most of us made at least three dives each day, except for Chuck, who I think made every dive. He always had a camera in his hand and was intent on shooting his own footage, but I remember he also took the time to offer us tips on how to get better photos and videos.

That trip proved to be the start of many great adventures shared with Chuck and Roz. I've been a scientific diver for more than 40 years, but it was Chuck who reintroduced me to the fun of recreational diving.

From Mentor to Model

By Mary Lynn Price

I met Chuck at the Diving Locker not long after his son Terry taught me to scuba dive. My work as a trial attorney with the San Diego County Office of the Public Defender was a world away from the underwater realm, although when I signed up for one of Chuck's shark diving trips to the Bahamas I recall him making a joke about sharks and attorneys and professional courtesy. You've probably heard that one …

Anyway, before that trip I'd never touched a video camera. But when Chuck handed me his camera during a dive, I was hooked. It changed my life.

From then on, Chuck was my mentor in all things video. I traveled with him as often as I could to places like Papua New Guinea, Chuuk, the Coral Sea, the Great Barrier Reef, the Maldives, Fiji, Tonga, Thailand, Burma, the Red Sea, and Lembeh in Indonesia. And there was that time we did a night dive together off La Jolla looking for a mysterious lobster. (Chuck doesn't particularly care for night dives—except in Lembeh!)

We used to have a dive club with the Diving Locker, the Nautilus Club. There were a handful of us very interested in learning more about video and sharing tips and approaches. With Chuck's enthusiastic encouragement our small group of highly motivated video shooters decided to start an underwater film festival. The San Diego Underwater Film Exhibition became real in 2000, when Chuck, myself, Bob Gladden and Steve Douglas dug into our pockets and came up with enough money to rent the Otto Theater at the San Diego Zoo for one night. It was a great success. This film exhibition continues to this day as a 501(c)(3) non-profit organization, and is considered one of the most prestigious in the country. We've kept to our original philosophy of no entry fees, no prizes (except a coffee cup), affordable tickets, and the honor of having your film selected and shared with a very appreciative audience.

It is Chuck's way to share with and encourage others, and by sharing his knowledge he has helped many people become better filmmakers. His contribution to the underwater imaging community is extraordinary.

One of my favorite times with Chuck was when we traveled to Chuuk and Chuck's luggage and camera gear didn't arrive for a couple of days. I had the great pleasure of diving with my friend and mentor Chuck as my model—even if it was only because he had no camera equipment! He proved to be as skilled a model as he is a cameraman.

Wine-Drunk with Whales

By Andy Pruna

When I think of whales, I always think of Chuck. When I think of California, I always think of Chuck. When I think of my wife, well Chuck doesn't always come to my mind, but almost. Why, you ask? Well, most of my diving with whales, particularly my first-ever dive with whales was with Chuck more than 40 years ago—and like they say, you always remember the first time.

I met Chuck in the late 1960s when I was in California as part of the US Navy's Sealab III program. What struck me the most was his happy, easygoing personality. In all the years I've known him I have never seen Chuck appear sad. Ever since, I have linked California with Chuck. To me, he is the embodiment of California—or maybe how California should be.

Finally, I met my wife in the remote Patagonian region of southern Argentina when Chuck and I were working together on a *National Geographic* film shoot. I remember him telling me he thought I was crazy to fall for a girl who lived at the end of the world. But still, he gave me his blessing. Sort of. Well, 43 years have passed and Marisabel, who is my wife, is still with me.

There are really so many different fond memories to tell involving Chuck, but a short anecdote that I will never forget was a time in 1976 or thereabouts when we where in Peninsula Valdes in southern Argentina, filming right whales. The weather was not exactly ideal for diving; the so-called "Patagonian breeze" was blowing its usual 30+ knots, so instead of diving we decided to go to an *azado*—an Argentine barbecue—which included roasted lamb and wine. Lots of wine. While the wind blew, we ate and drank like there was no tomorrow. After a while, Chuck came over to me and said, "Andy, I think the wind is dying down. Maybe we should go take a look at the sea conditions in the gulf," so we drove to a nearby cliff overlooking the bay. To our surprise, we saw a group of whales resting on the surface in the shallows. I remember the water appeared to be exceptionally calm and clear.

Within minutes we were out of our "wine fog" and into our wet suits. My memory of how we actually got into the water is hazy, but I vividly recall staring into the eye of a right whale. The massive whale remained motionless as I approached. Soon I found myself picking little crablike creatures—sea lice—from around its eye. (Had I not been "fortified" by wine I doubt I'd have had the nerve to do such a thing.) The whale could have easily thrashed me, but it kept still. They say God looks after fools and drunks. Maybe whales do, too …

I looked back once and noticed Chuck had approached, camera rolling. He gave me a quick thumbs up and smiled. He'd just captured some of the best footage we ever got.

The Only Person in the Room

By Adam Ravetch

I first met Chuck in 1980. I was a newly certified diver, who, along with a couple hundred other marine enthusiasts was attending an evening film festival held by the Underwater Photographic Society. And while I didn't actually meet Chuck in person that night, his dramatic film presentation—underwater footage of massive two-ton bull sea lions charging his camera—reached out to me as if I was the only person in the room. I still remember it vividly. I left the auditorium that night on a natural high, excited by Chuck's work and the other presenters— including Stan Waterman and San Diego's own Ozzie Wissel—feeling fortunate to have found this new world of diving, and wondering where it would take me if I stayed with it.

Two years later, I was deep into my dive training at San Diego State University and I landed a job at Chuck Nicklin's dive shop working in regulator repair. One of my intentions of working there was to actually meet Chuck, but he was gone on a filming trip that summer so I decided to learn as much as I could, and immerse myself in the waters off San Diego every chance I got. One day, I found myself alone in the shop on a rare slow business day, when in walks Chuck. He was just back from one of his great underwater filming adventures. There I was, face to face with Chuck Nicklin. And overcome with shyness that left me barely able to whisper a faint hello. Chuck recognized my awkwardness, introduced himself, and broke the ice with a casual, "Hey Tiger please do me a favor and fix my regulator," dropping it in my lap. Moments later, Chuck's son Flip walked in. He had just returned from one of his *National Geographic* magazine assignments to someplace glorious and exciting. He'd brought photos of schooling hammerhead sharks that he had just captured and was eager to share them with Chuck. I remember sitting there, just the three of us. I couldn't believe I was in the room with these two famous watermen, listening to them regale their incredible stories of adventure in the wilds from father to son, and from son back to father. I went home that night and decided that one way or another, I wanted to be like the Nicklins and pursue my passion for the oceans.

Of course, I still had a lot to learn. And Chuck continuously offered his support. On the eve of becoming a scuba instructor, I asked Chuck if I could borrow his underwater slides of lobsters walking on the seafloor, to give my final lecture about night diving an added punch. "No problem," he said. The slides were mine to use.

More than 25 years have passed since then. Inspired by the Nicklins, I went on to become a wildlife filmmaker. And when I consider where my filming career has taken me, I can't help but feel fortunate to have found my way to San Diego, to SDSU, and to the doorstep of Chuck Nicklin's dive shop.

The Sleeping Prince of Arabia

By Howard Rosenstein

I met Chuck for the first time around the mid- to late-1970s when he was a guest of a *National Geographic* expedition to the Red Sea led by Dr. Eugenie Clark and photographers David and Anne Doubilet. At the time, I owned and operated Red Sea Divers, the first dive operation in Sharem el Sheikh, Sinai, which was then under Israeli administration having been captured by Egypt in the 1967 Six Day war.

As soon as he arrived, Chuck won the hearts of our entire team with his laid-back California cool, movie star looks and incredible diving skills.

At the southern tip of the Sinai Peninsula, Sharm el-Sheikh was about as far away as one can get from La Jolla, not only in physical miles but also because it was really remote, primitive in creature comforts often compared to the "wild west" for it rugged individuals and landscape.

Yet underwater it was considered to be one of the truly great diving locations in the world.

Chuck loved diving the Red Sea and this one trip led to a friendship that has lasted over 40 years.

I remember one particular adventure like it was yesterday. We were working on a story about the flashlight fish, which involved a lot of night diving. Our "dive boat" was a small skiff, not much more than a pregnant paddleboard with an outboard engine strapped to it. By the time we loaded our gear—including David Doubilet's 10 massive housed camera rigs—the gunnels were just inches above the water line.

One night we hit a storm while returning from a dive. The wind blew hard and the seas picked up. We lashed the gear in place as best we could, but I was truly concerned that a big wave might wash one of us overboard into the night, so I started calling out each team member's name, "David?"

"Here."

"Anne?"

"Here."

"Genie?"

"Here."

"Chuck? Chuck? Chuck?!"

I heard nothing except the sound of the wind—and of my own now-racing heartbeat. I asked David to turn his powerful dive light on, thinking we were going to need to search for him adrift in the waves. But as David scanned the gear section with his light, there was Chuck, curled into a fetal position atop a pile of gear bags, sound asleep. I marveled at how anyone could fall asleep under these conditions, but apparently, as we learned later, Chuck is a master. He can sleep anywhere, any time—and under any conditions! Too cool, this guy.

After this trip, I visited Chuck in California and stayed at his bachelor pad on Eads Street off La Jolla cove. Chuck played gracious host to so many of his friends in the international diving community who knew they were welcome to pop in anytime for a soak in the hot tub, a great meal or a place to crash for the night. I had a wonderful visit and he even convinced me to risk a heart attack diving in the chilly California waters off the Coronado Islands—the first and only dry suit adventure for this Red Sea diver.

Chuck had the Diving Locker in those years and was the king of diving in San Diego, especially for organizing trips for his many clients and friends. He believed in the Red Sea as a great destination and over the years he brought many groups to dive with us in Sharem el Sheikh. When Israel signed the peace treaty with Egypt and the Sinai was returned to Egyptian sovereignty, Chuck actually wrote a personal letter to Israeli Prime Minister Begin and Egyptian President Anwar Sadat, pleading for the continuation of Red Sea diving tourism and protection of the Red Sea's coral reefs.

Just before we left the Sinai, we found a shipwreck rumored to have belonged to Lawrence of Arabia and sunk while laden with gold to pay off the Arab fighters aiding the British against the Turks. When the BBC expressed interest in making a documentary about our discovery, we insisted that Chuck come over from California to shoot the film. The result was a program titled, "Mystery of the Red Sea Wreck" made in 1979. It's a masterful work and you'll occasionally see it turn up on the Discovery Channel and other networks.

Part of the Gang

By Marty Snyderman

When I got hired to work at Chuck Nicklin's Diving Locker in the spring of 1975 I barely had two dimes to rub together. I was a brand new diving instructor, and looking back at that, I feel fairly certain that I was about the least qualified card-carrying instructor in the history of our sport.

I suspect I was as eager to become part of the Diving Locker gang as anyone who had ever come aboard. Maybe Chuck saw that in me and liked it. Or maybe I am flattering myself because Chuck was just a good guy to everyone that worked at the shop. I don't know. But I can tell you about my experience.

About a month after I started working at the shop I got elbowed in the jaw in a pick-up basketball game, leaving my face bruised and swollen. Naturally, I got teased. But looking back at it, taking that shot in my grille could have been one of the best things that ever happened to me.

Chuck joined in on all of the good-natured teasing. But just to be sure I didn't take it to heart, the next week on my day off a blue Porsche pulled into the driveway of the apartment I was renting in Pacific Beach. Unannounced, out jumped Chuck Nicklin!

Chuck had just returned from serving as a cinematographer on the Hollywood blockbuster, *The Abyss*. I had seen pictures floating around the shop of him hanging with people who have their names on the marquees at movie theaters. People who win Oscars and Emmys. What the hell was he doing at my apartment?

I barely knew Chuck. I had no idea what to think. I wondered if I was about to get fired. I remind you, I was so broke I could have put all my money in my socks and still got my shoes to fit my feet. The only piece of furniture to my name was a mattress. No box springs. No dresser drawers. No kitchen table. But I owned my dive gear.

Chuck rang my doorbell. But I was too embarrassed about the way I was living to answer the door. I stayed quiet and didn't move, waiting for Chuck to drive away.

The next day I was scheduled to work in the shop, and I went to work wondering if I had a job. A few minutes after I clocked in Chuck approached me and asked if I was, in fact, living where he thought I was. I confirmed my address. And then Chuck told me he had dropped by yesterday to see if I wanted to go to La Jolla Cove where a bunch of people were getting together for some volleyball and a picnic. He said he was sorry that I wasn't home, and he apologized for not having given me some advanced notice because it was a last-minute thing.

Are you kidding me? The owner, the cinematographer, the Hollywood hotshot had dropped by in his hot ride to see if I might want to join the gang. Well, that was, and is, Chuck!

Over the next couple of years while I worked at the Diving Locker, Chuck loaned me camera gear and routinely shared his photographic knowledge. Before long he asked me to tag along on a handful of shark shoots in the open sea off San Diego just because I expressed an interest. Although Chuck told me he invited me because I had so little experience in the diving world that I was his most expendable employee. That was Chuck too!

I watched Chuck closely when he was in the water surrounded by a bunch of sharks. Doing that helped me learn how to dive relaxed and be smart, or at least smarter, diving in the open sea around blue sharks and mako sharks. Those days were incredibly beneficial to me at that stage of my diving career. Do your part, pay attention, never bitch about anything, and Chuck would invite you again. That's Chuck.

One day a bunch of the Diving Locker gang got together to jump out of an airplane. It was something I had always wanted to do, and I was one of the organizers. Chuck really didn't seem to like the fact that so many of us went at one time. One of our store managers broke an ankle that day, and Chuck, half-kiddingly, but only half, told me it was too bad it wasn't me. After all, I was the most expendable member of the group. A few months later I got promoted to being the manager of the Escondido Diving Locker. Chuck again!

So yes, like a lot of the guys that worked at the Diving Locker, and a lot of the guys that dived with the shop, I, too, wanted to be just like Chuck when I grew up. But in my case it wasn't just because Chuck caught the attention of the ladies, and because he was the underwater photographer and cinematographer I wanted to become someday. I wanted to be like Chuck because he was simultaneously a diving icon, and just one of the guys. He wanted everyone to have fun and feel like part of the gang.

Forty years later I see the exact same qualities in Chuck when I go to the San Diego Underwater Video Club meetings. Chuck is happy to share his work, experience and enthusiasm with the accomplished shooters and the newbies alike. Come one, come all. Just come on and get in the game. That's why 40 years ago I said, "When I grow up, I want to be like Chuck."

I still do.

The Dive Buddy
Who Has My Back

By Karen Straus

For the 40-plus years I have known Chuck Nicklin, he has been helping me out of tight spots. Literally.

The first tight spot was about as literal as you can get. In the early 1970s Chuck and I were part of a film team working on a documentary about Palau, its marine life and unique Rock Islands. The film, produced, directed and photographed by renowned cinematographer Al Giddings, was called The Sea of Eden. The short documentary, shown on the film festival circuit and as an in-flight movie on Continental Airlines and its subsidiary, Air Micronesia, helped set Palau on the path to becoming a world-class diving destination and UNESCO World Heritage Site.

But in the early '70s, when Chuck, Al and I were working in Palau on film and photography assignments, Palau was in its infancy as a dive and tourism destination. There was a lot of exploring to do, pioneering dive sites such as Blue Corner, German Channel and Jellyfish Lake, sites at the time known only to locals and airline crew who were divers. Chuck, Al and I were among the very first to dive Blue Corner and to swim in Jellyfish Lake. Today, these sites attract many thousands of divers annually.

The first few times Chuck, Al and I visited Jellyfish Lake, we arrived at the Rock Island by small boat. To get to the lake, we hiked into the densely vegetated interior over a steep trail lined with jagged, razor-sharp limestone outcroppings. It was hot, buggy work carrying all of our scuba gear and topside and underwater camera equipment to the lake.

At the time, little was known about the marine lake and the masses of specialized, stingless, Golden Jellyfish living there. One of the questions was how the jellies got there in the first place. Jellyfish are typically marine critters; the marine lake was an enclosed body of mostly fresh water with no visible connection to the seawater lagoon surrounding the island.

The photograp010her Douglas Faulkner, who spent years living in and documenting Palau in his exquisite photo book, *This Living Reef*, shared information with us about Palau's marine lakes, including the time he was photographing jellies and noticed in his peripheral vision a large log floating on the surface. As he lowered the camera to look at the log, he realized that the log had eyes and was looking right back at him. As Doug told it, "The photograp010her in me raised the camera up and started to turn the focus knob, but another part of my brain activated my feet and propelled me backwards, away from the crocodile." Doug made it safely out of the lake, with a newly developed respect for crocodiles.

With Doug's story fresh in our minds, Al announced that he wanted to film a sequence proving that Jellyfish Lake was somehow connected to the outlying salt lagoon, perhaps via an underwater tube or siphon. Sure, Chuck and I said, thinking of that big croc, and wondering how IT got in and out of the lake, never mind the jellyfish.

Conferring with locals, we located a siphon that might connect Jellyfish Lake to the lagoon. We were advised that the only possible time to explore the siphon would be slack tide. Otherwise we ran the very real risk of becoming trapped in the siphon by powerful tidal flows. The slack tide window allowed us a very limited amount of time in which to explore the siphon.

With Al and an assistant going in first with the film camera and movie lights, Chuck and I climbed down into the siphon. A safety diver brought up the rear. Al would more or less navigate through the siphon shooting back as Chuck and I crawled and swam toward him, the team emerging (hopefully) out the other end into daylight and Jellyfish Lake. Or would the siphon be a dead end? Nobody knew.

Did I mention that parts of the siphon were a pretty tight squeeze? To give you an idea of what parts of it were like, try belly crawling across the floor wearing full-ocean gear. Now try it over sharp and slippery limestone rocks, your stomach squashed against the rocks underneath and your tank valve and head bumping the rock ceiling above. Some of the time we crawled and swam submerged in water; other times we crouched and crawled our way through air and water chambers.

I should mention here that it was pretty darn dark in there, except for the dive lights Chuck and I carried and Al's movie lights. And we didn't know where the crocodile might be. Were we inadvertently crawling into his lakeside lair? Nobody knew the answer to that one, either.

After what seemed like an interminable amount of time, and with the water flow definitely picking up, we could just make out a dim blue-green light ahead, and it wasn't Al's movie lights. With a final push, we crawled out of the siphon, relieved to see daylight again and delighted be swimming freely in the open waters of Jellyfish Lake. At this point, we could have cared less if a croc was frolicking alongside us.

We did some crazy things back in the day, didn't we? I could not have done the siphon crawl without Chuck. His courage, calmness and professionalism gave me the confidence to "go with the flow," so to speak. I knew that Chuck had my back, and that was good enough for me.

Many years later, in 2009, Chuck had my back again in another hair-raising tight spot, when my husband, the photographer-writer Eric Hanauer, suffered decompression sickness while we were diving in Baja, California, Mexico. Eric and I were attending a family wedding in Cabo San Lucas. My cousin invited us on a dive, and off we went to Gordo Banks, a single dive that morning, the wedding that evening. Four of us made the same dive profile, all of us used dive computers, none of us got into deco, all of us made safety stops, Eric came up bent.

There I was in Mexico, with Eric in the recompression chamber in Cabo and elderly parents attending the wedding with me. The first phone call I made was to DAN for medical advice; the second call was to Chuck and Roz Nicklin, back home in San Diego. After letting them know about Eric's spinal bends hit and prognosis, I asked if I could send my parents home on the next flight, and if they could meet them at the airport and get them back to their San Diego home. Chuck and Roz did not hesitate a second. They drove to the airport late at night, picked up my folks, drove them home, and checked on them until Eric and I were able to return to San Diego a week later, after Eric had completed six chamber treatments and was cleared by DAN to fly.

Happily, not every story with Chuck is a hair-raising, tight squeeze situation! In 2007, Eric and I traveled to Palau with Chuck, Roz and 30 friends to help Chuck celebrate his 80th birthday. The festivities took place topside and underwater, culminating in a group underwater photo complete with an underwater birthday cake. Organizing 30 divers underwater for a group portrait without stepping on any corals was almost as challenging as swimming through the Jellyfish Lake siphon all those years ago. But Eric managed to herd the divers into place and get the birthday picture, Chuck front and center, surrounded by his dive buddies.

The Man Who Loves Cats

By JoRene and Gunars Valkirs

We moved to Maui in 2007 after living in San Diego. While in San Diego, we didn't know Chuck, but since we had several occasions to visit a Diving Locker, it's possible we may have had a brief conversation with him, but not that we recall.

It wasn't until 2009 when we met. The meeting happened at our front door in Maui. Chuck's son, Flip Nicklin arranged for them to stay with us for several days while attending an event called Whale Quest.

Flip Nicklin is one of the founders of a research organization called Whale Trust. Each year the Whale Quest event is held to present the latest whale research to the public. We had started a family foundation prior to our move to Maui. Shortly after the move we learned of Whale Quest and became one of its sponsors. When Flip asked if we'd be willing to host his father and Roz at our home for a few days, we didn't hesitate. Little did we know we were about to meet a fearless man, one with a secret talent.

Those who know Chuck most likely know him as a bold adventurer, one who has spent a great portion of his life underwater; a person with a life of excitement and wonder who views the world that exists beneath sea level. We, on the other hand, discovered a humble, soft-spoken guy who loves cats.

Chuck and Roz have now stayed with us several times since that first visit. I remember the first time they arrived at our home, our dogs were clamoring for their attention. However, when we mentioned we also had a cat, I saw Chuck's eyes lit-up. We introduced Chuck to our calico, Peanut—but with a warning. Peanut was once a feral kitten and has never been fully domesticated. She's not what you'd call a "nice kitty." During her early years, she would hide behind doors and spring out, ambushing us as we walked by, her ears pinned back, tail twitching and claws bared. I held out my arms to show Chuck some of my scars. Peanut has mellowed a bit with age, but I always feel like I have to warn my guests, just in case she decides to turn back into a feral attack cat.

Chuck was undaunted, showing the fearlessness of a man who swims with sharks. I held my breath as his outstretched hand reached for the cat. I waited for the familiar hissing sound. But no such thing happened. Instead, there came a loud purring noise as Peanut moved closer to Chuck, nudging him, allowing him to stroke behind her head.

So now you know. The man who sat on a whale, the man who bravely swims with sharks? He's nothing compared to the man who won the affection of a feral cat.

Nicklinites

By Alison Vitsky Sallmon

I moved to San Diego long after Chuck sold the Diving Locker, many years after he inspired the countless divers and photographers that passed through its doors. At that time I'd been diving for over a decade but underwater photography hadn't interested me at all. Until I met Chuck Nicklin. Well, to be honest, I hadn't actually met him yet, but here's where our story begins.

As an avid diver, I subscribed to a lot of diving magazines, including one called *Fathoms*. That's where I first met Chuck—or at least learned his name. Even though I had exactly zero interest in underwater photography, a feature article about Chuck Nicklin and his career as an underwater photographer and filmmaker just captivated me. I still have no idea why that article stood out to me, but not long after that I impulsively blew a huge chunk of money on a used dSLR camera rig—the camera, housing, strobes, the whole deal. And with no clue how to use it. I dove constantly and tried so hard with that camera and read everything I could get my hands on, but I didn't feel like my photography would ever improve. I secretly wondered if that money would have been better spent on something more grown up and responsible, like furniture.

One day, I attended a local underwater photographic society meeting and there was Chuck Nicklin, sitting in the front row. I kept attending the meetings (after all, Chuck's presence seemed like a pretty big stamp of approval for attendance), but I was pretty shy about sharing my images with other members. One day, Chuck said something complimentary about an image of mine in front of the whole club. I pushed aside my shyness and walked right up to him after the meeting and thanked him, told him how much I appreciated his comment—

and his kindness. After that, he would occasionally make comments to me about my photography, pointing out what he liked and offering constructive criticism and tips on how I might improve my imaging. I finally felt like I was starting to learn something. The kicker, though, came a year or so later when I ran into Chuck and Roz at a local dive shop. That's when Chuck looked at me and said, "You have an eye." It was the first time someone had said something like that to me, and everything fell into place. Even though I still couldn't afford to buy new furniture, I finally felt certain that my impulsive "What am I doing?" camera splurge had been the right decision. I will never forget that day.

Of course, you have probably realized by now that my "Chuck story" isn't terribly original. In fact, I'd be way far back in a long line of underwater shooters whom Chuck has inspired, influenced—and encouraged.

Chuck is very well known for motivating the people who worked for him at his store, but his effect on new photographers did not stop when the Diving Locker changed hands. You cannot attend any film festival or photographic society show in California (and probably much farther afield) without hearing that Chuck has inspired someone, that Chuck has mentored someone, that Chuck has had an influence on someone's work. I wonder if Chuck has any idea of the massive legacy in his wake: We are huge in number—an Army of Nicklinites!

Tinkering Around

By Bruce Wight

I met Chuck through my girlfriend, who is now my wife. She had just received her scuba certification at the Diving Locker and signed us up for a trip with Chuck to Palau. Needless to say, it was a fantastic trip that has led to a long friendship. We've traveled with Chuck and Roz to many other places since then.

In addition to our friendship, one of the reasons we like to travel with Chuck is that he exudes an infectious enthusiasm about a destination that invites the curious and adventurous traveler. That, and Chuck's many years of experience as a world travel makes him especially qualified to plan and lead trips.

One of the things I admire about Chuck is how he stays current on emerging technology within the world of underwater photography and filmmaking. It's not easy to do, as things go from "new and improved" to "obsolete and out of stock" in what seems like minutes. Instead of appearing confounded by it, Chuck seems challenged. I enjoy seeing his new camera gear and hearing the passion in his voice as he speaks of what he has his sights on next.

I've certainly benefited from his pursuit of high-tech gear. Under Chuck's influence I finally made the switch from film to digital. And on our last trip I packed up my drone camera system and hauled it to Fiji. Shooting footage with my drone was one of the highlights of my trip. The locals enjoyed it, too.

Neither of us are real big talkers, but we're both avid tinkerers. I enjoy creating camera accessories in my garage and many of my gadgets are based on Chuck's ideas, which are usually conjured up during an occasional breakfast get together and quickly sketched on a napkin. Some of the best ideas are born this way, you know. We've had fun tinkering around putting these ideas to the test, and in this way we enjoy one another's company, too.

You'll not hear Chuck brag about his accomplishments. He'd much rather talk about his future plans than reminisce about the "good old days." This is rare. And it's why I'm so pleased he's finally written a book.

Final Thoughts

The Fun of "Unretirement"

The work of a freelance cameraman is sporadic. You might have work that lasts a few days or be on location for a few months and then have no work at all for a while. It's just the nature of the business.

One of the main reasons I was able to make a living as a cameraman, especially in the early days, is that I always had the Diving Locker to fall back on. I hired good managers and had a staff that looked after things while I was off shooting a film. After finishing *The Abyss* I thought I could always go back to the Diving Locker, but things were changing. By this time my son Terry was working in the real estate business and Flip had a steady gig as a *National Geographic* photographer. Without the family involvement, the business seemed to be losing its place in the industry. We'd had the Diving Locker for 42 years. We decided it was time to sell.

We sold it to a person who thought he knew everything about the sport and business side, but it wasn't long before we took it back and sold it again. This time we sold it to a young man who thought the diving business would be a lot of fun. Before long he learned it meant a lot of hard work and long hours. Now, the Diving Locker is no more.

When we first sold it I said, "I am retired." That lasted a few days before I realized that retirement sucks and isn't for me.

Werner Kurn, owner of Ocean Enterprises, had been a friendly competitor and had built a growing dive/travel business. After my retirement from the Diving Locker, we had lunch and discussed merging my travel business with Ocean Enterprises. This marked my "unretirement." Just like we'd done at the Diving Locker for many years, Roz and began running trips through Ocean Enterprises. And it's been a lot of fun. Werner and his wife, Myra have the best diving operation in the country and it's been our pleasure for many years to organize dive and safari travel through Ocean Enterprises.

A "Family Meeting"

How fortunate I am that my two sons, Flip and Terry, who are extensions of my life, share my love of the water. They practically grew up at the beach and were always in the water, just like me when I was a kid.

Both were accomplished freedivers, who as teens were into spearfishing competitions and were Junior Pacific Coast Champions. They helped out at Chuck's Market and then later when we had the Diving Locker they became scuba instructors and worked in all phases of the business. Terry managed the Diving Locker before becoming a successful real estate salesman. Flip's work as a photographer led to his career at *National Geographic*. Both are fine men whose company I enjoy. I'm proud of them.

Years ago Terry helped Flip with an assignment photographing sperm whales in Sri Lanka. It was their first time working with sperm whales.

It just so happened that I was in Sri Lanka at the same time, filming *Whales Weep Not* with Rick Rosenthal. Rick and I had been following a pod of sperm whales for hours when we finally had a chance to approach them. After a lengthy swim I dived on a perfect set up. As I was filming, all the sudden I notice a pair of divers in the background. It was my sons. Wrecking my shot. When I surfaced and got over my initial frustration of having them get in my way, I had to laugh. I mean, what are the odds of all three of us being in the exact same spot in the ocean at the same time, filming that exact same pod of whales?

I called them over to me and we had a "family meeting" about staying out of each other's shots—or more importantly—about them staying out of my shots.

Connecting the Dots

Writing this book has given me plenty of time to reflect on my life and adventures. When I look back, I realize that so many seemingly unrelated events shaped my life—from carefree childhood days at the lake to the struggles of the Great Depression and World War II—so I thought I'd take a moment to revisit my earlier years.

I was born on September 3rd, 1927, at my grandmother's house on Midland Street in Worcester, Massachusetts. My parents named me after my father, Charles Richard Nicklin. My brother Frances Law Nicklin was born three years later, and then the next year my sister, Elsie Mae Nicklin arrived.

We moved to Northboro, a small town about 30 miles west of Boston. Our little two-story house on Hudson Street with brown shingles was set apart from the other houses in the neighborhood, and a river ran about a hundred yard behind the house, so we had plenty of room to explore. It was the perfect place for youngsters to grow up.

Many of my happiest childhood memories are of times spent on the water. If we weren't on the river we were at my uncle's place on Lake Quinsigamond. We spent a lot of time there, swimming, and boating on the lake.

Like many American families, our family struggled through the Great Depression. My dad lost his job. He did whatever it took to keep food on the table, taking odd jobs to make ends meet. Dad eventually got hired by the Work Projects Administration (WPA) as part of the New Deal, which was a federal program initiated to help ease the burden of the Depression.

I was just a kid at the time, but I got a job at the grocer, making 10 cents an hour pulling weeds.

In 1938, my father joined the Naval Reserve and at the start of World War II he was placed into active duty in the Navy. He was at sea for long periods, which was hard on all of us.

One day my father came home on leave and said we were moving to San Diego. That was someplace in California. It was far, far away. As far as I knew, it could have been the moon. I was a 14-year old teenager and I didn't want to go. I was the oldest—old enough to help out— but I was rebellious. My mom had to handle all the packing by herself. I regret that, but I was just a young kid…

We boarded the train for San Diego on New Year's Eve, in a snowstorm. My brother Fran and I were put in one car and my mother and sister Elsie were put in another car. I remember my mother panicking, fearing that we'd get separated. I don't blame her. We'd never been on a train, and here we were traveling all the way across the country.

We made it to San Diego without incident. My father met us there. It was the start of an entirely new life.

The entire West Coast was gearing up for the war, and there was lots of talk about a possible Japanese attack. I was going to school in Point Loma, and I remember studying the silhouettes of Japanese and German planes, especially bombers. That was the situation in San Diego in 1943.

This was when I started hanging out at the beach. It was amazing to stand on the cliffs in La Jolla and look into the clear water. I spent a lot of time walking along the cliffs at Bird Rock and La Jolla, learning to snorkel at La Jolla cove.

I graduated from high school in 1945 and joined the Navy. I was 17 years old. My plan was to become a fighter pilot, but that didn't really work out. The war in Europe had already ended, and the war in Japan came to an end while I was still in boot camp, so I

Camera Man

sort of missed out on the opportunity to be a famous World War II flying ace. I ended up training as a coxswain, which meant I'd have been assigned to pilot landing craft used to transport soldiers to shore during invasions. That would have been a job that could have gotten me killed fairly easily, so I'm fortunate that the war ended when it did. With the war over, the Navy didn't know what to do with us. We were given the choice to opt out of the Navy, so I did. My military career was short-lived, lasting only one year, one month, and one day.

I had been stationed in Hawaii, so I returned home to San Diego and enrolled as a student at San Diego State. Before I'd joined the Navy I was a typical La Jolla kid, hanging out at the soda fountain dressed in my Levi's, a t-shirt and huarache sandals. Esther Crosthwaite, the girl who worked the soda fountain, had a younger sister named Gloria. Gloria and I hit it off, but we never dated. One of the first things I did upon returning home was make contact with Gloria Crosthwaite. I remember our first date; I showed up at her house in my Navy uniform, thinking I was hot shit, with my dragon cuffs on my sleeves. Her father met me at the front door, took one look at me, and gave me a hard look. I feared he might slam the door in my face. Gloria was still in high school, and he didn't like the thought of his daughter going out with some Navy guy.

After leaving the Navy with an honorable discharge for war service that I didn't actually perform, I lived at home. My dad had retired and had a Navy housing unit on the hills in Pacific Beach. I bought a car. A 1935 Ford. It had no front fenders, but it was my car and I loved it. I was dating Gloria and going to school at San Diego State and was studying to be a chemist.

Gloria's father was in construction and did commercial diving. He was working in the Colorado River and doing hardhat diving, driving piles into the bottom. There was an accident and he drowned. His body was never recovered.

Gloria's grandfather had a small Mexican grocery store in Logan Heights, and after her father's death, her mother went to work at the store. She was struggling to manage the grocery business.

When I look back on it, this time in my life seems like it happened really fast. Gloria and I ran off and got married. We moved in with her mom and I went to work part-time helping at the grocery store early in the morning, while taking college classes during the day and working at a gas station at night. It wasn't long before Flip was born, followed 10 months later by Terry. All the sudden I was a family man. There weren't enough hours in the day and it seems like there was never enough money. I left college to work full time in the family grocery business and Gloria got a job at Merrill-Lynch.

Before long Gloria's mother became ill and wasn't able to manage the grocery store, so I went to work full-time as a grocer. I decided if it was going to be a full-time job for me, I wanted it to become my store. Everyone agreed and we changed the store from Crosthwaite's Market, to Chuck's Market. I am proud to say it's still in business, and still has the same name.

I learned to cut meat and how to make chorizo sausage. I learned how to buy vegetables and find the right potatoes and not buy the fruits that have bad ones on the bottom. I became a buyer. And I had customers come from all over. They were faithful customers because I always treated them right.

The grocery business wasn't easy. I worked long hours and it seems like there were always problems to sort out. But that's the way it is when you own a business and you have a family to provide for. I did whatever I needed to do to keep my head above water. And somehow I always managed to make time to go diving, and to share my love of the water with my sons Flip and Terry.

It might be hard for someone to connect the dots of my life story, from an abbreviated military career to running a grocery store to owning a dive shop to pursuing a career as an underwater photographer and filmmaker. It's hard for me to see how all this linked up—and I lived it.

If someone asked me to share the secret of my success, here's what I'd say:

Work hard, whether you're doing what you love or doing what you have to do.

Try not to complain.

Take lots of naps. Like my dad always said, "Don't stand up if you can sit down. Don't sit down if you can lie down. And don't stay awake if you can sleep."

And most of all, love the ones you love. And let them know you love them.

Filmmaking

The world of underwater photography and filmmaking has undergone several revolutions since it began, when in the early 1900s men like William Longley, William Beebe and Louis Boutan captured the first underwater images.

So many underwater explorers and photographers have been among the early pioneers that paved the way for others. It's impossible to mention the names of all who've helped bring the world of underwater photography to where it is today, so I won't try and do it here. But I will say that I'll always be grateful to the people who designed cameras and strobes and built housings and tested the limits on camera technology and pushed every new development past its limit to a new edge, and beyond.

Digital technology has made everything easier. And new camera systems just keep getting smaller and smaller, and the quality continues to improve. Today a kid with a GoPro can shoot better footage than Al Giddings and I got using the steamer trunk-sized Panavision camera we were hauling around in the 1960s.

It's all happened so fast.

One thing that's so exciting about all these new developments is that it makes underwater photography available to more people than ever before, who can create art and share it with others—especially those who don't dive—to help educate them about our fragile marine environments.

As I put the finishing touches on this book, I'm sitting on the porch at the Montana ranch owned by Al Giddings. As I have stated many times before, he has been an important part of my life in the film industry and we have shared a very long and strong friendship that continues today. This will be the last time I sit here and admire the view, as

Al is thinking of selling his ranch and moving back to California to concentrate on his passion of restoring antique autos.

Everything changes, and the film industry is no exception. I feel fortunate to have enjoyed a good career as a cinematographer. I hope that by sharing my stories I have given you a good glimpse of what it's been like.

It's been one helluva ride.

I'm grateful to all those who helped me along the way, and I feel lucky to have had a chance to help others pursue their goals as underwater photographers and filmmakers.

Thank you.